ALONE
WITH
GOD

ALONE
WITH
GOD

REDISCOVERING THE POWER
AND PASSION OF PRAYER

JOHN MACARTHUR

DAVID C COOK

transforming lives together

ALONE WITH GOD
Published by David C Cook
4050 Lee Vance Drive
Colorado Springs, CO 80918 U.S.A.

Integrity Music Limited, a Division of David C Cook
Brighton, East Sussex BN1 2RE, England

The graphic circle C logo is a registered trademark of David C Cook.

Unless otherwise noted, all Scripture quotations are taken from the *New American
Standard Bible*, © Copyright 1960, 1995 by The Lockman Foundation. Used by
permission. Scripture quotations marked NIV are taken from the Holy Bible, New
International Version®, NIV®. Copyright © 1973, 1978, 1984 by Biblica, Inc™. Used
by permission of Zondervan. All rights reserved worldwide. www.zondervan.com.

Library of Congress Control Number 2011926834
ISBN 978-0-7814-0586-7
eISBN 978-1-4347-6671-7

The Team: Alex Field, Sarah Schultz, Jack Campbell, Karen Athen
Cover Design: Amy Kiechlin Konyndyk
Cover Photo: iStockphoto 2613138

Printed in the United States of America
Third Edition 2011

7 8 9 10 11 12 13 14 15 16

111020

CONTENTS

INTRODUCTION

Martyn Lloyd-Jones once wrote, "Prayer is beyond any question the highest activity of the human soul. Man is at his greatest and highest when upon his knees he comes face to face with God."[1] Commentator J. Oswald Sanders had this lofty view of prayer:

> No spiritual exercise is such a blending of complexity and simplicity. It is the simplest form of speech that infant lips can try, yet the sublimest strains that reach the Majesty on high. It is as appropriate to the aged philosopher as to the little child. It is the ejaculation of a moment and the attitude of a lifetime. It is the expression of the rest of faith and of the fight of faith. It is an agony and an ecstasy. It is submissive and yet importunate. In the one moment it lays hold of God and binds the devil. It can be focused on a single objective and it can roam the world. It can be abject confession and

rapt adoration. It invests puny man with a sort of omnipotence.[2]

The essence of prayer is simply talking to God as you would to a beloved friend—without pretense or flippancy. Yet it is in that very attitude toward prayer so many believers have trouble. That is because communion with God is so vital and prayer so effective in the fulfillment of God's plan, the enemy attempts constantly to introduce errors into our understanding of and commitment to prayer. Every generation faces the necessity to reprioritize and purify a corrupted or confused perception of prayer. For many, prayer has been replaced with pragmatic action. Function overrides fellowship with God; busyness crowds out communication. For others, prayer lacks a sense of awe and respect. Their efforts are flippant, disrespectful, and irreverent. Then there are those who believe prayer is designed to make demands and claims on God. They attempt to force Him to do what they believe He should do for them. Finally, for some, prayer is nothing more than a routine ritual.

You may view prayer with the utmost respect, yet you find your own practice lacks purpose and vitality, so you don't spend time with God like you know you should. While there are many reasons Christians struggle to pray, I believe there is one overriding factor. Martyn Lloyd-Jones wrote:

> It is the highest activity of the human soul, and therefore it is at the same time the ultimate test of a man's true spiritual condition. There is nothing that tells the truth about us as Christian people so

much as our prayer life.... Ultimately, therefore,
a man discovers the real condition of his spiritual
life when he examines himself in private, when he
is alone with God.... And have we not all known
what it is to find that, somehow, we have less to
say to God when we are alone than when we are in
the presence of others? It should not be so; but it
often is. So that it is when we have left the realm of
activities and outward dealings with other people,
and are alone with God, that we really know where
we stand in a spiritual sense.[3]

Alone with God—such an opportunity should be the Christian's
one great desire. How sad that so many believers spend brief amounts
of time with Him, or don't go to Him at all, because they have so
little to say.

Many years ago when I preached through Matthew's gospel at
Grace Community Church, specifically chapter 6 and the portion
most commonly known as the "Lord's Prayer," it so revolutionized
people's praying that I took the opportunity to write a book on the
subject. Titled *Jesus' Pattern of Prayer,* it dealt exclusively with the
pattern Jesus set for prayer in Matthew 6, which is so foundational
to all our understanding of prayer.[4] This new edition, called *Alone
with God,* has allowed me the opportunity to publish it again with
David C Cook.

But this book is more than a simple revision of the chapters from
the original; I have also added several chapters made up of various
passages from the New Testament that should broaden and enhance

your understanding of prayer. While Jesus' pattern for prayer occupies the central portion of the book, you need to understand what the Holy Spirit–inspired New Testament writers built on that foundation.

The first part will examine the attitude all believers should have regarding their communication with God. All Christians ought to necessarily have their hearts focused on God so that communion with Him is an everyday, natural function of their lives. The first chapter will define and examine this vital need for us to be praying without ceasing. At the same time, we all need to guard against praying with the wrong attitude. That was what plagued the Pharisees, who viewed prayer as a means to show off their spirituality rather than as a humble opportunity to glorify God.

To correct the disciples' tainted perspective of prayer gleaned from those hypocritical religious leaders, Jesus offered a pattern that gave a comprehensive view of all the essential elements of righteous prayer, every one of which centers on God. This central portion of the book will cover each phrase of our Lord's pattern of prayer. From beginning to end, you'll discover that Jesus focuses our attention on God—on His adoration, worthiness, and glory.

To help you apply what you have learned, the final two chapters of the book will examine the specific things all believers should pray for. What you read may surprise you, for just as a father must correct his child's priorities in life, God must do the same with regard to our practice of prayer.

It is my prayer for you that when you have completed your journey through this book, you'll rediscover the power and passion that time spent alone with God can bring. I also hope you'll understand that prayer is not an attempt to get God to agree with you or provide for your selfish desires but that it is both an affirmation of His sovereignty, righteousness, and majesty and an exercise to conform your desires and purposes to His will and glory.

Part One

THE ATTITUDE OF PRAYER

1

A HEART SET ON GOD

For Christians, prayer is like breathing. You don't have to think to breathe because the atmosphere exerts pressure on your lungs and forces you to breathe. That's why it is more difficult to hold your breath than it is to breathe. Similarly, when you're born into the family of God, you enter into a spiritual atmosphere wherein God's presence and grace exert pressure, or influence, on your life. Prayer is the normal response to that pressure. As believers, we all have entered the divine atmosphere to breathe the air of prayer. Only then can we survive in the darkness of the world.

Unfortunately, many believers hold their spiritual breaths for long periods, thinking brief moments with God are sufficient to allow them to survive. But such restricting of their spiritual intake is caused by sinful desires. The fact is, every believer must be continually in the presence of God, constantly breathing in His truths to be fully functional.

Because ours is such a free and prosperous society, it is easier for Christians to feel secure by presuming on instead of depending on God's grace. Too many believers become satisfied with physical blessings and have little desire for spiritual blessings. Having become so dependent on their physical resources, they feel little need for spiritual resources. When programs, methods, and money produce impressive results, there is an inclination to confuse human success with divine blessing. Christians can actually behave like practical humanists, living as if God were not necessary. When that happens, passionate longing for God and yearning for His help will be missing—along with His empowerment. Because of this great and common danger, Paul urged believers to "pray at all times" (Eph. 6:18) and to "devote yourselves to prayer" (Col. 4:2). Continual, persistent, incessant prayer is an essential part of Christian living, and it flows out of dependence on God.

The Frequency of Prayer

Jesus' earthly ministry was remarkably brief: barely three years long. Yet in those three years, as must have been true in His earlier life, He spent a great amount of time in prayer. The Gospels report that Jesus habitually rose early in the morning, often before daybreak, to commune with His Father. In the evening, He would frequently go to the Mount of Olives or some other quiet spot to pray, usually alone. Prayer was the spiritual air that Jesus breathed every day of His life. He practiced an unending communion between Himself and the Father.

He urged His disciples to do the same. He said, "Keep on the alert at all times, praying that you may have strength to escape all these things that are about to take place" (Luke 21:36).

The early church learned that lesson and carried on Christ's commitment to continual, unceasing prayer. Even before the day of Pentecost, the 120 disciples gathered in the upper room and "with one mind were continually devoting themselves to prayer" (Acts 1:14). That didn't change even when 3,000 were added to their number on the day of Pentecost (2:42). When the apostles were led to structure the church so that ministry could be accomplished effectively, they said, "We will devote ourselves to prayer and to the ministry of the word" (6:4).

Throughout his life, the apostle Paul exemplified this commitment to prayer. Read the benedictions to many of his epistles and you'll discover that praying for his fellow believers was his daily practice. To the Roman believers he said, "God ... is my witness as to how unceasingly I make mention of you, always in my prayers making request" (Rom. 1:9–10; cf. 1 Cor. 1:4; Eph. 5:20; Phil. 1:4; Col. 1:3; 1 Thess. 1:2; 2 Thess. 1:3, 11; Philem. v. 4). His prayers for believers often occupied him both "night and day" (1 Thess. 3:10; 2 Tim. 1:3).

Because he prayed for them so continually, Paul was able to exhort his readers to pray that way as well. He urged the Thessalonians to "pray without ceasing" (1 Thess. 5:17). He commanded the Philippians to stop being anxious and instead "in everything by prayer and supplication with thanksgiving let your requests be made known to God" (4:6). He encouraged the Colossians to "devote yourselves to prayer, keeping alert in it with an attitude of thanksgiving" (4:2; cf. Rom. 12:12). And to help the Ephesians arm themselves to combat the spiritual darkness in the world around them, he said, "With all prayer and petition pray at all times in the Spirit, and with this in view, be on the alert with all perseverance and petition for all the saints" (6:18). Unceasing, incessant prayer is essential to the vitality of a believer's relationship to the Lord and his ability to function in the world.

A Way of Life

As a child, I used to wonder how anyone could pray without ceasing. I pictured Christians walking around with hands folded, heads bowed, and eyes closed, bumping into everything. While certain postures and specific times set aside for prayer have an important bearing on our communication with God, to "pray at all times" obviously does not mean we are to pray in formal or noticeable ways every waking moment. And it does not mean we are to devote ourselves to reciting ritualistic patterns and forms of prayer.

To "pray without ceasing" basically refers to recurring prayer, not nonstop talking. Thus it is to be our way of life—we're to be continually in an attitude of prayer.

Famous nineteenth-century preacher Charles Haddon Spurgeon offered this vivid picture of what praying at all times means:

> Like the old knights, always in warfare, not always
> on their steeds dashing forward with their lances
> in rest to unhorse an adversary, but always wear-
> ing their weapons where they could readily reach
> them, and always ready to encounter wounds
> or death for the sake of the cause which they
> championed. Those grim warriors often slept in
> their armour; so even when we sleep, we are still

to be in the spirit of prayer, so that if perchance we wake in the night we may still be with God. Our soul, having received the divine centripetal influence which makes it seek its heavenly centre, should be evermore naturally rising towards God himself. Our heart is to be like those beacons and watchtowers which were prepared along the coast of England when the invasion of the Armada was hourly expected, not always blazing, but with the wood always dry, and the match always there, the whole pile being ready to blaze up at the appointed moment. Our souls should be in such a condition that ejaculatory prayer should be very frequent with us. No need to pause in business and leave the counter, and fall down upon the knees; the spirit should send up its silent, short, swift petitions to the throne of grace.

A Christian should carry the weapon of all prayer like a drawn sword in his hand. We should never sheathe our supplications. Never may our hearts be like an unlimbered gun, with everything to be done to it before it can thunder on the foe, but it should be like a piece of cannon, loaded and primed, only requiring the fire that it may be discharged. The soul should be not always in the exercise of prayer, but always in the energy of prayer; not always actually praying, but always intentionally praying.[1]

I think of praying at all times as living in continual God consciousness, where everything we see and experience becomes a kind of prayer, lived in deep awareness of and surrender to our Heavenly Father. It is something I share with my Best Friend—something I instantly communicate with God. To obey this exhortation means that, when we are tempted, we hold the temptation before God and ask for His help. When we experience something good and beautiful, we immediately thank the Lord for it. When we see evil around us, we ask God to make it right and to allow us to help accomplish that, if it is according to His will. When we meet someone who does not know Christ, we pray for God to draw that person to Himself and to use us as faithful witnesses. When we encounter trouble, we turn to God as our Deliverer.

Thus life becomes a continually ascending prayer: All life's thoughts, deeds, and circumstances become opportunities to commune with our Heavenly Father. In that way, we constantly set our minds "on the things above, not on the things that are on earth" (Col. 3:2).

Fellowship with God

Since the ultimate purpose of our salvation is to glorify God and to bring us into intimate, rich fellowship with Him, failure to seek God in prayer is to deny that purpose. "What we have seen and heard we proclaim to you also," said the apostle John, "so that you too may have fellowship with us; and indeed our fellowship is with the Father, and with His Son Jesus Christ" (1 John 1:3).

Imagine spending an entire workday with your best friend at your side. You would no doubt acknowledge his presence throughout the day by introducing him to your friends or business associates and talking to him about the various activities of the day. But how would your friend feel if you never talked to him or acknowledged his presence? Yet that's how we treat the Lord when we fail to pray. If we communicated with our friends as infrequently as some of us communicate with the Lord, those friends might soon disappear.

Our fellowship with God is not meant to wait until we are in heaven. God's greatest desire, and our greatest need, is to be in constant fellowship with Him *now,* and there is no greater expression or experience of fellowship than prayer.

In one of his classic works on prayer, *Purpose in Prayer,* nineteenth-century pastor E. M. Bounds provided us with this reminder of how we must cultivate our fellowship with the Lord:

> Prayer is not a meaningless function or duty to be crowded into the busy or the weary ends of the day, and we are not obeying our Lord's command when we content ourselves with a few minutes upon our knees in the morning rush or late at night when the faculties, tired with the tasks of the day, call out for rest. God is always within call, it is true; His ear is ever attentive to the cry of His child, but we can never get to know Him if we use the vehicle of prayer as we use the telephone, for a few words of hurried conversation. Intimacy requires development. We can never know God as it is our privilege to know Him, by brief and fragmentary and unconsidered repetitions of intercessions that are requests

for personal favors and nothing more. That is not the way in which we can come into communication with heaven's King. "The goal of prayer is the ear of God," a goal that can only be reached by patient and continued and continuous waiting upon Him, pouring out our heart to Him and permitting Him to speak to us. Only by so doing can we expect to know Him, and as we come to know Him better we shall spend more time in His presence and find that presence a constant and ever-increasing delight.[2]

The Ways and Means of Prayer

In Ephesians 6:18, Paul says we are to pray with "all prayer and petition." The Greek word translated "prayer" (also in 1 Thess. 5:17) is the most common New Testament word for prayer and refers to general requests. The word translated "petition" refers to specific prayers. Paul's use of both words suggests our necessary involvement in all kinds of prayer, every form that is appropriate.

The Posture

To pray all the time necessitates being in various positions, because you will never be in the same position all day. In the Bible, people prayed while standing (Gen. 24:12–14), lifting up their hands (1 Tim. 2:8), sitting (Judg. 20:26 NIV), kneeling (Mark 1:40), looking upward (John 17:1), bowing down (Ex. 34:8), placing their heads between their knees (1 Kings 18:42), beating their breasts (Luke 18:13), and facing the temple (Dan. 6:10).

The Circumstances

While some people today think prayer ought to be very formal, the Bible documents that people prayed in many different circumstances. They prayed while wearing sackcloth (Ps. 35:13), sitting in ashes (Job 1:20–21; 2:8), crying tears (Ps. 6:6), throwing dust on their heads (Josh. 7:6), tearing their garments (1 Kings 21:27), fasting (Deut. 9:18), sighing (Ps. 6:4–6), groaning (Ezra 9:4–15), crying out loud (Heb. 5:7), sweating blood (Luke 22:44), agonizing with broken hearts (Ps. 34:18), making a vow (Acts 18:18), making sacrifices (Ps. 20:1–3), and singing songs (Acts 16:25).

The Place

The Bible records people praying in all sorts of places as well: in battle (2 Chron. 13:14–15), in a cave (1 Kings 19:9–10), in a closet (Matt. 6:6), in a garden (Matt. 26:36–44), on a mountainside (Luke 6:12), by a river (Acts 16:13), by the sea (Acts 21:5–6), in the street (Matt. 6:5), in the temple (1 Kings 8:22–53), in bed (Ps. 4:3–4), in a home (Acts 9:39–40), in the stomach of a fish (Jonah 2:1–10), on a housetop (Acts 10:9), in a prison (Acts 16:23–26), in the wilderness (Luke 5:16), and on a cross (Luke 23:33–34, 46). In 1 Timothy 2:8, Paul said, "I want the men in every place to pray." For the faithful, Spirit-filled Christian, every place becomes a place of prayer.

The Time

At a pastors' conference I attended some years ago, one man preached on the subject of morning prayer. To support his point, he read various passages that show people praying in the morning.

As he did, I looked up all the Scriptures that show people praying three times a day (Dan. 6:10), in the evening (1 Kings 18:36), before meals (Matt. 14:19), after meals (Deut. 8:10), at the ninth hour or 3:00 p.m. (Acts 3:1), at bedtime (Ps. 4:4), at midnight (Acts 16:25), day and night (Luke 2:37; 18:7), often (Luke 5:33), when they're young (Jer. 3:4), when they're old (Dan. 9:2–19), when they're in trouble (2 Kings 19:3–4), all day long (Ps. 86:3), and always (Luke 18:1; 1 Thess. 5:17).

Prayer is fitting at any time, in any posture, in any place, under any circumstance, and in any attire. It is to be a total way of life—an open and continual communion with God. After having embraced all the infinite resources that are yours in Christ, don't ever think you're no longer dependent on the moment-by-moment power of God.

Coincidental Attitudes

Throughout his life, the believer senses his insufficiency; thus he lives in total dependence on God. As long as you feel that insufficiency and dependence on God, you will pray without ceasing. At the same time, you also know you are the beneficiary of tremendous blessings from God. That's why Paul instructed the Thessalonians to "rejoice always" and "give thanks" in everything in their unceasing prayers (1 Thess. 5:16–18). That reflects a beautiful balance in our communion with God. While we offer specific petitions for our needs and the needs of others, at the same time we can rejoice and give thanks—not just for His specific answers, but also for the abundant blessing He pours out to us each and every day.

Fervency in Prayer

Since communication with God is to occur throughout the day, don't imagine that precludes the need for passion in your prayers. Paul commanded the Colossians, "Devote yourselves to prayer, keeping alert in it" (4:2), and he warned the Ephesians to "be on the alert with all perseverance and petition" as they prayed (6:18). For prayer to accomplish what God wants in our lives, it must be an all-consuming practice that makes alertness and perseverance its most valuable commodities.

Alertness

In its most basic sense, Paul's command to keep alert means to stay awake and not fall asleep during prayer. In Gethsemane shortly before His betrayal, Jesus asked Peter, James, and John to keep watch while He prayed (Matt. 26:38). He returned soon after only to find them already asleep, so He said to Peter, "So, you men could not keep watch with Me for one hour? Keep watching and praying that you may not enter into temptation; the spirit is willing, but the flesh is weak" (vv. 40–41). It is impossible to pray while sleeping—you must be awake and alert to talk to God, just as you are when talking with anyone.

Paul's instruction, both in Colossians 4:2 and Ephesians 6:18, encompasses more than mere physical alertness, however. Believers should also look for those things they ought to be praying about. Evidently Peter learned this deeper truth from his failure to stay awake, for he wrote in his first epistle, "Be of sound judgment and sober spirit for the purpose of prayer" (4:7).

Christians sometimes pray vague, general prayers that are difficult for God to answer because they do not really ask for anything specific. That's why specific prayer is so important. While general requests can be appropriate in certain instances, it is through His answers to specific prayers that we see God put His love and power on display. Jesus promised, "Whatever you ask in My name, that will I do, so that the Father may be glorified in the Son. If you ask Me anything in My name, I will do it" (John 14:13–14).

Those believers who continually seek the Lord have specific concerns; if you are not alert to the specific problems and needs of other believers, you can't pray about them specifically and earnestly. But when you do, you can watch for God's answer, rejoice in it when it comes, and then offer Him your thankful praise.

Perseverance

Unfortunately, most believers never get serious about prayer until a problem occurs in their lives or in the life of someone they love. Then they are inclined to pray intently, specifically, and persistently. But Paul says we are to always pray that way and to "be on the alert with all perseverance" (Eph. 6:18). The Greek word translated "perseverance" and in the command "devote yourselves" (Col. 4:2) is from *proskartereō*, a compound word made up of *kartereō* ("to be steadfast" or "to endure") and an added preposition that intensifies the meaning. The verb means "to be courageously persistent," "to hold fast and not let go." It is used of Moses' faithful endurance when he led the children of Israel out of Egypt (Heb. 11:27). To be devoted to prayer is to earnestly, courageously, and persistently bring everything, especially the needs of others, before God. Sensitivity to the problems and needs of others, including other believers who are facing trials and hardships, will lead us to pray for them "night and day" as Paul did for Timothy (2 Tim. 1:3).

Our Lord's Example

Jesus Himself was the epitome of perseverance in prayer. Hebrews 5:7 says, "In the days of His flesh, He offered up both prayers and supplications with loud crying and tears to the One able to save Him from death." That verse is a commentary on our Lord's prayer life while on earth—a life characterized by passionate prayers offered with great intensity and agony. Although Scripture does not chronicle the details of His prayers, we can be sure that He persevered in them, even if it took all night (Luke 6:12).

The greatest illustration of His intensity in prayer took place in the garden prior to His death. Luke wrote, "He knelt down and began to pray, saying, 'Father, if You are willing, remove this cup from Me; yet not My will, but Yours be done.' ... And being in agony He was praying very fervently; and His sweat became like drops of blood, falling down upon the ground" (22:41–42, 44). In Matthew's version of this same event, we find that Jesus petitioned God three times (26:36–46). That was one fervent, prolonged prayer experience, so much so that during it the disciples fell asleep several times.

Our Lord performed many mighty works when He was on earth, yet in none of them is there any apparent expenditure of energy. Although the Scripture says virtue went out of Him, there is no record that would indicate He had to exert any effort to perform His miracles. Only when He prayed do we see Him agonize and toil over His petitions, even to the point of sweating great drops of blood. Such persistence is foreign to us, yet it is that kind of intensity Christ wanted the disciples to learn from two parables He taught them.

Our Lord's Parables

Among the many parables of our Lord, two stand out as different from the others. While the other parables relate to God by comparison, those He gave in Luke 11 and 18 relate to God by contrast. They illustrate people who are unlike God, and in so doing, these parables make a strong case for the value of persistent praying.

> He said to them, "Suppose one of you has a friend, and goes to him at midnight and says to him, 'Friend, lend me three loaves; for a friend of mine has come to me from a journey, and I have nothing to set before him'; and from inside he answers and says, 'Do not bother me; the door has already been shut and my children and I are in bed; I cannot get up and give you anything.' I tell you, even though he will not get up and give him anything because he is his friend, yet because of his persistence he will get up and give him as much as he needs. So I say to you, ask, and it shall be given to you; seek, and you will find; knock, and it will be opened to you. For everyone who asks, receives; and he who seeks, finds; and to him who knocks, it will be opened." (Luke 11:5–10)

> Now He was telling them a parable to show that at all times they ought to pray and not to lose heart, saying, "In a certain city there was a judge who did not fear God and did not respect man. There was

a widow in that city, and she kept coming to him, saying, 'Give me legal protection from my opponent.' For a while he was unwilling; but afterward he said to himself, 'Even though I do not fear God nor respect man, yet because this widow bothers me, I will give her legal protection, otherwise by continually coming she will wear me out.'" And the Lord said, "Hear what the unrighteous judge said; now, will not God bring about justice for His elect who cry to Him day and night, and will He delay long over them? I tell you that He will bring about justice for them quickly." (Luke 18:1–8)

The contrast between God and the reluctant friend and unjust judge is obvious. If such unwilling and sinful humans will honor persistence, how much more will our holy, loving Heavenly Father? If you don't get an immediate answer to your request, or if events don't turn out exactly or as quickly as you hoped they would, our Lord's word to us is, "Don't lose heart." Just keep praying without ceasing and don't give up. Keep knocking. Keep asking. Keep seeking.

Spurgeon offered this insight to the importance of our persistence:

If we would prevail, we must persist; we must continue incessantly and constantly, and know no pause to our prayer till we win the mercy to the fullest possible extent. "Men ought always to pray." Week by week, month by month, year by year; the conversion of that dear child is to be the father's main plea. The bringing in of that unconverted husband is to lie upon the wife's heart night and day till she gets it; she is not to take even ten or twenty years of unsuccessful prayer as a reason why she should cease; she is to set God no times nor seasons, but so long as there is life in her and life in the dear object of her solicitude, she is to continue still to plead with the mighty God of Jacob. The pastor is not to seek a blessing on his people occasionally, and then in receiving a measure of it to desist from further intercession, but he is to continue vehemently without pause, without restraining his energies, to cry aloud and spare not till the windows of heaven be opened and a blessing be given too large for him to house. But, brethren, how many times we ask of God, and have not because we do not wait long enough at the door! We knock a time or two at the gate of mercy, and as no friendly messenger opens the door, we go our ways. Too many prayers are like boys' runaway knocks, given, and then the giver is away before the door can be opened. O for grace to stand foot to foot with the angel of God, and never, never, never relax our hold; feeling that the cause we plead is one in which we must be successful, for souls depend on it, the glory of God is connected with it, the state of our fellow men is in jeopardy. If we could have given up in prayer our own lives and the lives of those dearest to us, yet the souls of men

> we cannot give up, we must urge and plead again
> and again until we obtain the answer.[3]

When Paul commands us to pray without ceasing, he is simply supporting the principle Jesus taught in Luke 11 and 18 that prayer is to be incessant. We are not heard for our many words but for the cries of our hearts. The man who came to his friend to ask for bread did not recite some formula request; he pleaded for what he needed. The same is true for the widow—she cried out for protection to one who had the power to answer her request. Persistent, continual prayer that comes from the innermost part of your being is what moves the heart of our compassionate, loving God.

Power

The most important and pervasive thought Paul gave about prayer was that it should be "in the Spirit" (Eph. 6:18; cf. Jude v. 20). This qualification has nothing to do with speaking in tongues, nor with some other ecstatic or supernatural activity. To pray in the Spirit is to pray in the name of Christ—that is, to pray consistent with His nature and will. To pray in the Spirit is to pray in complete agreement with the Spirit, who "helps our weakness; for we do not know how to pray as we should, but the Spirit Himself intercedes for us with groanings too deep for words [real words unuttered, not non-words uttered]; and He who searches the hearts knows what the mind of the Spirit is, because He intercedes for the saints according to the will of God" (Rom. 8:26–27). Zechariah 12:10 calls the Holy Spirit the "Spirit of grace and of supplication." Just as we are to pray continually, know that the Holy Spirit continually prays for us. When we pray in the Spirit, we align our minds and desires with His mind and desires, which are consistent with the will of the Father and the Son.

How do you make your prayers consistent with the Spirit? By walking in the fullness of the Spirit. As your life is filled with the Spirit (Eph. 5:18) and as you walk in obedience to Him, He will govern your thoughts so your prayers will be in harmony with His. As you submit to the Holy Spirit, obey His Word, and rely on His leading and strength, you will be drawn into close and deep fellowship with the Father and the Son.

Our lives must reflect a continual commitment to the constant exercise of prayer. All that you learn about God should drive you into His presence. Make that your goal as you take every aspect of your life to Him in prayer.

2

SEEKING THE LORD IN SECRET

The greatest danger to persistent, effective prayer is the habit of performance without passion. Seventeenth-century Puritan pastor John Preston captured the essence of this danger in these words:

> If it is performed in a formal or customary and overly manner, you would be as good to omit it altogether; for the Lord takes our prayers not by number but by weight. When it is an outward picture, a dead carcass of prayer, when there is no life, no fervency in it, God does not regard it. Do not be deceived in this, it is a very common deception. It may be a man's conscience would be upon him, if he should omit it altogether. Therefore, when he does something, his heart is satisfied, and so he grows worse and worse. Therefore, consider that the

very doing of the duty is not that which the Lord heeds, but He will have it so performed that the end may be obtained and that the thing for which you pray may be effected.

If a man sends his servant to go to such a place, it is not his going to and fro that he regards, but he would have him to dispatch the business. So it is in all other works. He does not care about the formality of performance, but he would have the thing so done that it may be of use to him. If you send a servant to make a fire for you, and he goes and lays some green wood together and puts a few coals underneath, this is not to make a fire for you. He must either get dry wood, or he must blow until it burns and is fit for use.

So when your hearts are unfit, when they are like green wood, when you come to warm them and to quicken them by prayer to God, it may be you post over this duty, and leave your hearts as cold and distempered as they were before. My beloved, this is not to perform this duty. The duty is effectually performed when your hearts are wrought upon by it, and when they are brought to a better tune and temper than they were before.

If you find sinful lusts, your business there is to work them out by prayer, to reason the matter, to expostulate the thing before the Lord, and not to give over until you have set all the wheels of your soul right, until you have made your hearts perfect with God. And, if you find your hearts cleaving too much to the world, you must wean them and take them off. If you find a deadness and unaptness, an indisposition in you, you must lift up your souls to the Lord and not give over until you are quickened. And this is to perform the duty in such a manner as the Lord accepts, otherwise it is hypocritical performance; for this is hypocrisy, when a man is not willing to let the duty go altogether, nor yet is willing to perform it fervently, and in a quick and zealous manner.

He that omits it altogether is a profane person, and he that performs it zealously, and to purpose, is a holy man; but a hypocrite goes between both. He would do something at it, but he will not do it thoroughly. And, therefore, if you find you have carelessly performed this duty from day to day, that you have performed it in a negligent, perfunctory manner, know that it is a hypocritical performance. Therefore, when we spend so much time exhorting you to a constant course in this duty, remember still that you must perform it in such a manner that may have heat and life in it, that it may be acceptable to God.[1]

Sadly, all believers can relate in some degree to Preston's indicting words. Nothing is so sacred that Satan will not invade it. In fact, the more sacred something is, the more he desires to profane it. Surely few things please him more than to come between believers and their Lord during the sacred intimacy of prayer. Sin will follow us into the very presence of God; and no sin is more powerful or destructive than pride. In those moments when we would come before the Lord in worship and purity of heart, we may be tempted to worship ourselves. Martyn Lloyd-Jones wrote:

> We tend to think of sin as we see it in rags and in the gutters of life. We look at a drunkard, poor fellow, and we say, there is sin. But that is not the essence of sin. To have a real picture and understanding of sin, you must look at some great saint, some unusually devout and devoted man, look at him there on his knees in the very presence of God. Even there self is intruding itself, and the temptation is for him to think about himself, to think pleasantly and pleasurably about himself and to really be worshipping himself rather than God. That, not the other, is the true picture of sin. The other is sin, of course, but there you do not see it at its acme, you do not see it in its essence. Or to put it in another form, if you really want to understand something about the nature of Satan and his activities, the thing is not to go to the dregs or the gutters of life. If you really want to know something about Satan, go away to that wilderness where our Lord spent forty days and forty nights.

That's the true picture of Satan, where you see him
tempting the very Son of God.[2]

Sin leads us to take shortcuts in all the Christian disciplines, and
when we succumb to its temptation often enough, hypocrisy becomes
the pattern of our lives without our realizing it. Because hypocrisy
is such a subtle and destructive danger to vital Christian living, our
Lord was quick to condemn its many adherents. During His earthly
life, the group guiltiest of it was the Jewish religious leaders—those
whom you would normally expect to be His greatest supporters were
actually His greatest enemies. That's because His righteous words
and deeds condemned their own unrighteous practices. To protect
His followers from their evil influence, Jesus said, "Beware of the
leaven of the Pharisees, which is hypocrisy" (Luke 12:1).

The Pharisees, through their rabbinic tradition, had succeeded
in corrupting and perverting all the good things God had taught
the nation of Israel, including their practice of prayer. No religion
has ever had a higher standard and priority for prayer than Judaism.
As God's chosen people, the Jews were the recipients of His written
Word, "entrusted with the oracles of God" (Rom. 3:2). No other
people as a race or as a nation has ever been so favored by God or had
such direct communication with Him.

The Jewish Perspective on Prayer

Old Testament Jews desired to pray because they believed God wanted
them to approach Him. They didn't fear God the way pagans did their
gods. In fact, the rabbis said that the Holy One yearns for the prayers

of the righteous. They undoubtedly got that truth from Psalm 145:18, which says, "The LORD is near to all who call upon Him" (cf. Ps. 91:15). No true Jew with a right spirit ever doubted God's priority for prayer. The rabbis rightly believed prayer was not only communication with God but also a mighty weapon that released His power.

The Essence of Their Understanding

The Word of God makes clear that God wanted to hear the prayers of the people. Psalm 65:2 says, "O You who hear prayer, to You all men come." The Midrash, a Jewish commentary on portions of the Old Testament, says this about Psalm 65:2: "A mortal man cannot grasp the conversation of two people speaking at the same time, but with God it is not so. All pray before Him, and He understands and receives all their prayers" (*Rabbah* 21.4). Men may become tired of listening to people, but God's ears are never satiated; He is never wearied by men's prayers.

The Jewish teachers went even further, teaching the people to pray constantly and avoid the habit of praying only when they were desperate. The Talmud, the codification of rabbinic traditions, says, "Honour the physician before you have need of him.... The Holy One says, just as it is my office to cause the rain and the dew to fall, and make the plants to grow to sustain man, so art thou bounden to pray before me, and to praise me in accordance with my works; thou shalt not say, I am in prosperity, wherefore shall I pray? But when misfortune befalls me then will I come and supplicate" (*Sanhedrin* 44b). That is the right perspective. Prayer was not to be used just for emergency appeals; it was to be an unbroken conversation built around a living, loving fellowship with God.

The Elements of Their Prayers

The Jews believed their prayers should incorporate the following elements:

Loving Praise

The psalmist said, "I will bless the LORD at all times; His praise shall continually be in my mouth" (Ps. 34:1). Psalm 51:15 says, "O Lord, open my lips, that my mouth may declare Your praise."

Gratitude and Thanksgiving

Jonah said, "I will sacrifice to You with the voice of thanksgiving" (Jonah 2:9). In a relationship with the God of heavenly resources, there will always be something to thank Him for.

Reverence

The Old Testament saints didn't flippantly rush into God's presence, treating Him as if He were a man. They came before Him with reverence, recognizing that when they prayed, they were coming face-to-face with Almighty God. The prophet Isaiah saw the Lord in a vision "sitting on a throne, lofty and exalted, with the train of His robe filling the temple" (6:1). His response was, "I am a man of unclean lips, and I live among a people of unclean lips; for my eyes have seen the King, the LORD of hosts" (v. 5).

Patient Obedience

Old Testament Jews believed it was wrong to pray if their hearts were not right. Psalm 119 affirms that throughout its 176 verses. A true Jew had no reservations—he approached God with a spirit of obedience, desiring to please Him.

Confession

Godly Old Testament Jews knew that they were unclean and that when they came before God in prayer, they had to purge themselves of sin. That was David's perspective when he said, "Who may ascend into the hill of the LORD? And who may stand in His holy place? He who has clean hands and a pure heart" (Ps. 24:3–4). Only those who have dealt with their sins have the right to enter God's presence.

Unselfishness

The Jews had a sense of solidarity that we don't understand. They were national—a theocracy ruled by God. That Israel still exists as a nation shows how vitally they have clung to the preservation of that national identity. As a result, their prayers encompassed the good of the community and were not isolated to the individual. For example, the rabbis asked God not to listen to the prayer of a traveler. That's because he might pray for an easy journey with good weather and accommodating skies when the people in that vicinity actually needed rain for their crops.

Many of us come to God with personal pronouns in our prayers: *I, me,* and *my.* We tell the Lord about our needs and problems without thinking of others in the body of Christ. But we need to be willing to sacrifice what seems best for ourselves because God has a greater plan for the whole.

Humility

A true Jew went before the Lord in prayer to submit himself to the will of God. The greatest illustration of that came from the heart of the truest Jew who ever lived: Jesus. In His prayer in the garden of Gethsemane, He said to the Father, "Not My will, but Yours be done" (Luke 22:42). When we pray, instead of asking the Lord to do our will, we should conform ourselves to His will. We are to ask Him to work His will through us and give us the grace to enjoy it.

Perseverance

True believing Old Testament Jews taught that prayer was to be persistent. After the children of Israel had worshipped the golden calf, Moses prayed for forty days in a row that God would forgive them (Deut. 9:25–26). He persevered in prayer.

The Rabbinic Perversion of Prayer

In spite of such a great heritage of prayer, several faults subtly crept into Israel's prayer life (as identified by William Barclay in his helpful discussion in *The Gospel of Matthew*).[3]

Prayer Became Ritualized

The wording and forms of prayer were set, and they were then simply read or repeated from memory. Prayers easily became a routine, semiconscious religious exercise, able to be recited without any mental or passionate involvement by the individual.

The most common formalized prayers were the *Shema* (a composite of selected phrases from Deut. 6:4–9; 11:13–21; and Num.

15:37–41) and the *Shemonēh ʾesray* ("The Eighteen"), which incorporated eighteen prayers for various occasions. Both prayers were to be offered every day, regardless of where the people were or what they were doing. Faithful Jews even prayed all eighteen prayers of the *Shemonēh ʾesray* each morning, afternoon, and evening.

Three basic attitudes characterized the people who offered formalized prayers. Those Jews who had sincere hearts used the time of prayer to worship and glorify God. Some approached it indifferently, perfunctorily mumbling their way through the words as quickly as possible. Others, like the scribes and Pharisees, recited the prayers meticulously, making sure to enunciate every word and syllable perfectly.

Prescribed Prayers

The Jews developed prayers for every object and occasion, including light, darkness, fire, rain, the new moon, travel, good news, and bad news. I'm sure their original intent was to bring every aspect of their lives into God's presence, but they undermined that noble goal by compartmentalizing the prayers.

By limiting prayer to specific times and occasions, the Jews turned prayer into a habit that focused on a prescribed topic or situation, not on genuine desire or need. In spite of that, some faithful Jews like Daniel used those times as reminders to approach God in sincerity with a pure heart (Dan. 6:10).

Long Prayers

The religious leaders esteemed long prayers, believing that a prayer's sanctity and effectiveness were in direct proportion to its length. Jesus warned of the scribes who "for appearance's sake offer long prayers" (Mark 12:40). While a long prayer is not necessarily insincere, it does lend itself to dangerous tendencies like pretense, repetition, and rote. We are subject to the same temptations today, all too often confusing verbosity with meaning and length with sincerity.

Meaningless Repetitions

One of the Jews' worst faults was adopting the pagan religions' practice of meaningless repetition, just as the prophets of Baal in their contest with Elijah "called on the name of Baal from morning until noon," even raving "until the time of the offering of the evening sacrifice" (1 Kings 18:26, 29). Hour after hour they repeated the same phrase, trying by the quantity of their words and the intensity with which they were spoken to make their god hear and respond.

To Be Seen and Heard by Men

While the other faults are not necessarily wrong in themselves, having simply been carried to extremes and used in meaningless ways, the desire to use prayer as an opportunity to parade one's spirituality before men is intrinsically evil because it both originates in and is intended to satisfy pride. As we noted earlier in this chapter, the motive of sinful self-glory is the ultimate perversion of prayer. It robs prayer of its primary purpose: to glorify God (John 14:13).

The Condemnation by Christ

In Matthew 6:5–8, in the midst of His discussion of the contrast between true and false righteousness, Jesus condemned the Pharisees' practice of prayer in two specific areas: self-centered prayer and prayer that had no meaning. Each area manifests one or more of the faults that had so corrupted true prayer in the life of the nation.

Self-Centered Prayer

Since pride was at its root, our Lord first dealt with those who prayed to exhibit their supposed spirituality before men. "When you pray, you are not to be like the hypocrites; for they love to stand and pray in the synagogues and on the street corners so that they may be seen by men. Truly I say to you, they have their reward in full" (Matt. 6:5). Prayer that focuses on self is always hypocritical because every true prayer focuses on God.

The term *hypocrite* originally referred to Greek actors who wore masks that portrayed in exaggerated ways the roles they were dramatizing. Thus hypocrites are pretenders—persons who are playing a role. The only thing you truly know about them is the false image that disguises their real beliefs and feelings.

The False Audience: Men

The hypocritical scribes and Pharisees prayed for the same reason they did everything else: to attract attention and bring honor to themselves. That was the essence of their righteousness, which Jesus said had no part in His kingdom (Matt. 5:20).

On the surface, Jesus' condemnation of their practice of prayer seems unwarranted. Certainly there was nothing wrong with standing and praying in the synagogues. Standing was the most common position for prayer in first-century Israel, and the synagogues were the most appropriate and logical places for public prayers to be offered. As long as the prayer was sincere, it was suitable. Even the practice of praying at the "street corners" was not wrong in itself—that was actually a normal place for prayer. At the appointed hour for prayer, devout Jews would stop wherever they were, even if they were walking along the street.

The real evil of these hypocritical worshippers, however, was not the location of their prayers but their desire to display themselves "so that they may be seen by men." The Greek word for *street* refers to a wide, major street and the street's corner. The scribes and Pharisees made a point of praying where a crowd was most likely to gather. Whatever place might afford the largest audience, that's where you would find these hypocrites.

In their desire to exalt themselves before their fellow Jews, the scribes and Pharisees were guilty of pride. They were like the Pharisee in Jesus' parable, who "stood and was praying this to himself" (Luke 18:11). God had no part in their pious activity. As a result, they had "their reward in full." Since they were concerned only about the reward men could give, that's all they received.

It's imperative we take to heart Jesus' warning in Matthew 6:5. To develop intimacy with anyone requires openness and sincerity, and that certainly applies to our relationship with God. If you ever want to experience power and passion in your communication with the Lord, you must begin by making sure your motives are like those of the publican in Luke 18:13–14, who approached God with a humble and penitent attitude.

The True Audience: God

In contrast to the hypocritical practice of the day, Jesus instructed His followers: "When you pray, go into your inner room, close your door and pray to your Father who is in secret, and your Father who sees what is done in secret will reward you" (Matt. 6:6). Notice that the Lord gave no prescribed time or occasion for prayer. All He said was, "When you pray," thus giving us great latitude to pray at all times.

To make as great a contrast as possible between God's pattern for prayer and that which was practiced by the scribes and Pharisees, Jesus said that when you pray, "go into your inner room." That could refer to any small room or chamber, even a storage closet. Such rooms were often secret and used to store and protect valuables. But Jesus' point was not about the proper location to pray; rather, it was about attitude. If the true worshipper found it necessary, he should find the most secluded, private place available to avoid the temptation to show off. When he got there, he should close the door to keep out all distractions, so he could concentrate on God and pray to Him and Him alone.

I will never forget one day when my oldest son, Matthew, was only five years old. I was walking down the hall of our home when I heard his voice coming from our bedroom. I couldn't quite make out what he was saying, so I moved to a spot just outside the room. No one was in the room with him. He was lying on our bed praying. He had something on his heart that he wanted to say to God, so he went to a room all alone and prayed. It didn't matter to him that no one could see him because he wasn't talking to an audience; he was talking honestly with God.

Much of our prayer lives should take place literally in secret. Jesus regularly left His disciples so He could find places to be alone as He prayed. Our family and friends may be aware of times when we are praying, but what we say is meant for God, not them. Certainly there are occasions when public prayer also edifies those who hear because it represents their feelings and needs. But even those prayers convey a certain intimacy because God is the focus of the requests. When a person's heart is right and concentrated on God, public prayer will in a profound way close one up alone in the presence of God, making it no different in motive than a prayer offered in the most private of places.

When we pray with the right attitude, "[our] Father who sees what is done in secret will reward [us]." The most important secret He sees is not the words we say in the privacy of our rooms, but the thoughts we have in the privacy of our hearts. Those are the secrets He is most concerned about. And when He sees that He is the true focus of our prayers, we will receive the reward only He can give. Jesus doesn't tell us what that reward will be, but we do know that God will faithfully and unfailingly bless those who come to Him in sincerity and humility.

Meaningless Prayer

The hypocritical prayers of the scribes and Pharisees were offered not only in the wrong spirit but also with meaningless words. They had no substance, no significant content. To be acceptable to God, prayers must be genuine expressions of worship and of heartfelt requests and petitions.

False Content: Meaningless Repetition

The practice of using meaningless repetition in prayer was common in many pagan religions in Jesus' day, as it is in many religions today. Thus His warning was clear: "When you are praying, do not use meaningless repetition as the Gentiles do, for they suppose that they will be heard for their many words" (Matt. 6:7). The phrase *use meaningless repetition* is the translation from the Greek text of one word that refers to idle, thoughtless chatter.

The Jews had picked up this practice from the Gentiles, who believed that the value of prayer was largely a matter of quantity, supposing "they [would] be heard for their many words." They believed their deities first had to be aroused, then cajoled, intimidated, and finally badgered into listening and answering.

Prayer was simply a matter of religious ceremony to the Gentiles, and it became that way for the Jews as well. Since no effort is required in those types of prayer, those who followed that practice could be totally indifferent to the prayer's content. But worse than that, they were indifferent to real communion with God.

Each of us would do well to heed our Lord's warning here. We have all been guilty of repeating the same prayers meal after meal and meeting after meeting—with little or no thought of God or what we are saying. Prayer that is thoughtless and detached is offensive to God and should be offensive to us.

Let me add one qualification, however. Jesus is not forbidding the repetition of genuine requests. In the first chapter, we looked at those verses that declare the value of persistent prayer. Honest, properly motivated repetition of needs or praise is not wrong. But the mindless, indifferent recital of spiritual-sounding incantations or magical formulas is.

True Content: Sincere Requests

In contrast to those who use meaningless repetition, Jesus said, "Do not be like them; for your Father knows what you need before you ask Him" (Matt. 6:8). God's purpose in prayer is not for us to inform or persuade Him to respond to our needs but to open sincere and continual lines of communication with Him. Prayer, more than anything else, is sharing the needs, burdens, and hungers of our hearts with a God who cares. He wants to hear us and commune with us more than we could ever want to commune with Him, because His love for us is so much greater than our love for Him.

How should you respond to these important words from our Lord? If you are ever to know power and passion in your prayer life, you need to pray with a devout heart—with a pure motive seeking only the glory of God. You also need to pray with a humble heart, seeking only the attention of God, not men. Finally, you need to pray with a confident heart, knowing full well that God already knows what you need. If you go to God on those terms, He will reward you in ways you could never imagine, and you'll learn the value of being alone with God.

Part Two

THE PATTERN OF PRAYER

3

"OUR FATHER"

Nineteenth-century pastor and author E. M. Bounds, who is well-known for his writings on the subject of prayer, said it best, "Prayer honors God; it dishonors self."[1] The scribes and Pharisees never understood that truth, and I fear the same is true for much of today's church.

The waves of our indulgent, selfish, materialistic society have washed ashore on Christian theology in many forms, including the prosperity gospel. Although the Bible teaches that God is sovereign and man is His servant, the prosperity gospel implies the opposite. Teaching that claims we can demand things of God is spiritual justification for self-indulgence. It perverts prayer and takes the Lord's name in vain. It is unbiblical, ungodly, and is not directed by the Holy Spirit.

Prayer begins and ends not with the needs of man but with the glory of God (John 14:13). It should be concerned primarily with who

God is, what He wants, and how He can be glorified. Those who teach otherwise are not preoccupied with the extension of Christ's kingdom or the glory of God's name but with the enlargement of their own empires and the fulfillment of their own selfish desires. Such teaching attacks the heart of Christian truth—the very character of God.

To believe that God is really like some genie, waiting to grant our every desire, flies in the face of Scripture's clear teaching. Many Old Testament saints certainly had just cause to plead with God to take them out of harrowing circumstances, yet they sought to glorify God and follow His will.

Recalling what happened while he was inside a great fish, Jonah said, "I remembered the LORD; and my prayer came to You, into Your holy temple.... I will sacrifice to You with the voice of thanksgiving. That which I have vowed I will pay. Salvation is from the LORD" (Jonah 2:7, 9). When Jonah seemingly had good cause to demand God to get him out of the fish, he simply extolled the character of God.

Daniel was often in dangerous situations because of his strategic role within the pagan Babylonian society. In his concern over Judah's captivity, he prayed, "Alas, O Lord, the great and awesome God, who keeps His covenant and lovingkindness for those who love Him and keep His commandments, we have sinned" (Dan. 9:4–5). He began his prayer by affirming the nature and character of God.

The prophet Jeremiah lived the majority of his life in frustration and confusion, all the while weeping with a broken heart over his people. While he could have easily despaired over his ministry, he never became preoccupied with his own painful circumstances. Instead he would pray and extol the glory, name, and works of God (e.g., Jer. 32:17–23).

Those Old Testament saints knew they were to recognize God in His rightful place and bring their wills into conformity with His. And that's just what Jesus taught the disciples when He said, "Pray, then, in this way" (Matt. 6:9). In fewer than seventy words, we find a masterpiece of the infinite mind of God, who alone could compress every conceivable element of true prayer into such a brief and simple form—a form that even a young child can understand but the most mature believer cannot fully comprehend:

> Our Father who is in heaven, hallowed be Your name. Your kingdom come Your will be done, on earth as it is in heaven. Give us this day our daily bread. And forgive us our debts, as we also have forgiven our debtors. And do not lead us into temptation, but deliver us from evil. For Yours is the kingdom and the power and the glory, forever. Amen. (vv. 9–13)

Jesus presented this prayer as a bold contrast to the substandard, unacceptable prayers common to the religious leaders of His day, which we considered in the last chapter. After warning the disciples of the perversion that had so corrupted Jewish prayer life, our Lord gave a divine pattern so all believers could pray in a way that is pleasing to God.

Jesus' Pattern for Prayer

This prayer, often called the "Lord's Prayer," when it could be more accurately titled the "Disciples' Prayer," is not a set group of words to repeat. When Christ said to "pray, then, in this way," He didn't mean to pray with His exact words. His intention was to give the disciples a pattern for the structure of their own prayers, especially since He had just warned them of the dangers of meaningless repetition. That doesn't mean we shouldn't recite it, as we do with so many passages in Scripture. Memorizing it is actually helpful so we can meditate on its truths as we formulate our own thoughts. The prayer is mainly a model we can use to give direction to our own praise, adoration, and petitions. It is not a substitute for our own prayers but a guide for them.

The initial benefit of this prayer is the way it exhibits the believer's relationship with God. "Our Father" presents the father-child relationship; "hallowed be Your name," the deity-worshipper; "Your kingdom come," the sovereign-subject; "Your will be done," the master-servant; "give us this day our daily bread," the benefactor-beneficiary; "forgive us our debts," the savior-sinner; and "do not lead us into temptation," the guide-pilgrim.

This prayer also defines the attitude and spirit we ought to have. "Our" reflects unselfishness; "Father," family devotion; "hallowed be Your name," reverence; "Your kingdom come," loyalty; "Your will be done," submission; "give us this day our daily bread," dependence; "forgive us our debts," penitence; "do not lead us into temptation," humility; "Yours is the kingdom," triumph; "and the glory," exultation; and "forever," hope.

In similar ways, the prayer can be outlined to emphasize the balance of God's glory and our need. It can also show the threefold purpose of prayer: to hallow God's name, to usher in His kingdom, and to do His will. And it details our present provision (daily bread), past pardon (forgiveness of sins), and future protection (safety from temptation).

No matter how perfect a pattern this is, we must remember our Lord's previous warning about our attitude in prayer. If our hearts are not right, even the Disciples' Prayer can fall into misuse. So how do you make sure you have the right heart attitude? Just make sure you focus on God. That's why this prayer is such a helpful model. Every phrase and petition focuses on God—on His person, His attributes, and His works. You prevent your prayers from being hypocritical or mechanical when you focus on God, not on yourself.

True prayer comes from humble people who express absolute dependence on God. That's what our Lord wants in our prayers. The more we think true thoughts about God, the more we will seek to glorify Him in our prayers. Commentator John Stott said, "When we come to God in prayer, we do not come hypocritically like play actors seeking the applause of men, nor mechanically like pagan babblers, whose mind is not in their mutterings, but thoughtfully, humbly and trustfully like little children to their Father."[2]

God Is Our Father

Father is probably the most common term we use in prayer, and rightly so, for that follows the pattern Jesus set. Prayer should always begin with the recognition that God is our Father, the One who gave us life and who loves, cares for, provides for, and protects us.

The fact that God is *our* Father means that only believers in Christ are children in His family. Admittedly, Malachi wrote, "Do we not all have one father? Has not one God created us?" (Mal. 2:10), and Paul did say to the Greek philosophers on Mars Hill, "As even some of your own poets have said, 'For we also are His children'" (Acts 17:28). But Scripture makes it perfectly clear that God is the Father of unbelievers only in creation.

Spiritually, unbelievers have another father. In His severest condemnation of the Jewish leaders who opposed Him, Jesus said, "You are of your father the devil" (John 8:44). First John 3 clearly characterizes two families: the children of God and the children of the devil. The former do not continue to commit sin; the latter do. The apostle Paul made a clear *distinction between* the children of light and the children of darkness (Eph. 5:8).

There is simply not just one spiritual family of mankind under one universal fatherhood of God. Second Peter 1:4 says that only those who believe have been made "partakers of the divine nature." It is only to those who receive Him that Jesus gives "the right to become children of God, even to those who believe in His name" (John 1:12). Thus we can go to God as His beloved children.

The Jewish Perspective of God

Whereas "our Father" declares a wonderful intimacy between God and His children, most of the world in Jesus' day worshipped gods who were characterized as distant and fearsome. That eventually became the Jewish perspective of God. Because of their continual disobedience to God throughout the centuries, including tolerating pagan gods, the Jews severed any true relationship they had with God as their Father. To them He had become little more than a relic of the past, a remote being who once called and guided their ancestors.

But those faithful Jews, both in our Lord's time and before, knew God as their Father. Isaiah saw Him that way. To deal with the nation's sinfulness, he prayed:

> You were angry, for we sinned, we continued in them a long time; and shall we be saved? For all of us have become like one who is unclean, and all our righteous deeds are like a filthy garment; and all of us wither like a leaf, and our iniquities, like the wind, take us away. There is no one who calls on Your name, who arouses himself to take hold of You; for You have hidden Your face from us and have delivered us into the power of our iniquities. But now, O LORD, You are our Father. (Isa. 64:5–8)

Isaiah reminded them of the comforting reality that God was their Father and that He would take care of them.

The Jews in the Old Testament saw five basic elements that encompassed the fatherhood of God.

As Father of the Nation

First Chronicles 29:10 gives God the title "LORD God of Israel our father." That identifies Him as Father of the nation.

As a Father Who Is Near

A father is closer than an uncle or a cousin or a friend or a neighbor. Psalm 68, while using dramatic language to refer to the grandeur of God's power, simply says that God is "a father of the fatherless" (v. 5).

As a Gracious Father

A father is forgiving, tenderhearted, merciful, and gracious to His children, which is very true of God: "Just as a father has compassion on his children, so the LORD has compassion on those who fear Him" (Ps. 103:13).

As a Guiding Father

A father leads his children and gives them wisdom and instruction. That was also true of God's relationship to Israel. He said of them, "With weeping they will come, and by supplication I will lead them; I will make them walk by streams of waters, on a straight path in which they will not stumble; for I am a father to Israel" (Jer. 31:9).

As a Father Who Requires Obedience

Because God was their Father, the people were required to obey Him. Deuteronomy 32:6 reiterates that: "Do you thus repay the LORD, O foolish and unwise people? Is not He your Father who has bought you?"

The Biblical Perspective of God

When Jesus arrived on the scene, He reintroduced His Jewish audience to God as a loving, beneficent Father to those who know, love, and obey Him. In the Sermon on the Mount, He taught them that the Father takes care of the needs of His children:

> Ask, and it will be given to you; seek, and you shall
> find; knock, and it shall be opened to you. For every-
> one who asks receives, and he who seeks finds, and

> to him who knocks it will be opened. Or what man
> is there among you who, when his son asks for a loaf,
> will give him a stone? Or if he asks for a fish, he will
> not give him a snake, will he? If you then, being evil,
> know how to give good gifts to your children, how
> much more will your Father who is in heaven give
> what is good to those who ask Him! (Matt. 7:7–11)

Jesus reaffirmed to them what their Scripture taught and what faithful, godly Jews had always believed: God is the Father in heaven to those who trust in Him.

In all His prayers, Jesus used the title *Father*, except when He was on the cross bearing the sin of the world and was forsaken by God (Matt. 27:46). Though the text of Matthew 6:9 uses the Greek word *Patēr*, Jesus likely used the Aramaic word *Abba* since that is the language He and the majority of Palestinian Jews commonly spoke. Since *Abba* is equivalent to our term *Daddy*, Jesus would have used it to emphasize the personal and intimate relationship God has with His children.

To be able to approach God in prayer as our loving Heavenly Father implies several things.

It Dispels Fear

Missionaries report that, because so many individuals live in fear of their gods, one of the greatest gifts Christianity ever brings to primitive societies is the certainty that God is a loving, caring Father. The invented false gods of false religions are typically characterized as vengeful and jealous, and their worshippers must take desperate measures to appease them. But knowing that the true God is our Father dispels all such fear.

It Encourages Hope

In the midst of a hostile world that's falling apart, God is our Father, and He'll take care of our future. If an earthly father will spare no effort to help and protect his children, how much more will our Heavenly Father love, protect, and help us (Matt. 7:11)?

It Removes Loneliness

Even if we are rejected and abandoned by family, friends, or even fellow believers, we know that our Heavenly Father will never leave us (Heb. 13:5). To drive away loneliness, God's presence is all a believer ever needs.

Paul Tournier, a Christian physician, wrote in his *A Doctor's Casebook in the Light of the Bible*:

> There was one patient of mine, the youngest daughter in a large family which the father found it difficult to support. One day she heard her father mutter despairingly, referring to her, "We could well have done without that one." That is precisely what God can never say. He is a loving Father to every one of His children.[3]

It Defeats Selfishness

Jesus included all of God's children in His pattern for prayer. This is evident in His plural-pronoun usage from the very first phrase, our Father, and on throughout the prayer. Jesus began with the words *our Father* because our prayers should embrace the entire community of the faithful. Remember that Ephesians 6:18 says we are to pray for "all the saints." We are to pray holding up to God what is best for all, not just for one.

It Provides Resources

God is "our Father who is in heaven." All the resources of heaven are available to us when we trust God as our heavenly supplier. He "has blessed us with every spiritual blessing in the heavenly places in Christ" (Eph. 1:3). Commentator Arthur W. Pink wrote:

> If God is in heaven then prayer needs to be a thing of the heart and not of the lips, for no physical voice on earth can rend the skies, but sighs and groans will reach the ears of God. If we are to pray to God in heaven, then our souls must be detached from all the earth. If we pray to God in heaven, then faith must wing our petitions.[4]

Whatever you seek, whether it's peace, fellowship, knowledge, victory, or boldness, God has an abundant supply in the heavenlies. We need only ask our Father for it.

It Demands Obedience

If Jesus, as God's true Son, came down from heaven not to do His own will but His Father's (John 6:38), how much more are we, as adopted children, to do only His will? Obedience to God is one of the supreme marks of our relationship to Him as children.

Yet in His grace, God loves and cares for His children even when they are disobedient. The story Jesus told in Luke 15 would be better titled the parable of the loving father rather than the prodigal son. The father in the story represents our Heavenly Father, who can forgive and rejoice over both a self-righteous son who remains moral and upright and a rebellious son who becomes dissolute, wanders away, but then returns.

When you begin your prayers by calling on "Our Father who is in heaven," you indicate your eagerness to go to Him as a child, knowing He loves you. And you'll find that He is eager to lend His ear, His power, and His eternal blessing to the requests of His children if it serves them best and further reveals His purpose and glory.

4

"HALLOWED BE YOUR NAME"

Throughout the centuries, no names have endured more abuse than those belonging to our Heavenly Father and His Son, Jesus Christ. Whether used in an epithet or curse, in casual or formal conversation, in secular or theological discussions, their names are more often treated with disrespect than with respect or exaltation. Martyn Lloyd-Jones offered this insightful perspective on how we use God's name:

> What unworthy ideas and notions this world has of God! If you test your ideas of God by the teaching of the Scriptures you will see at a glance what I mean. We lack even a due sense of the greatness and the might and the majesty of God. Listen to men arguing about God, and notice how glibly they use the term.... It is indeed almost alarming

to observe the way in which we all tend to use the
name of God. We obviously do not realize that
we are talking about the ever blessed, eternal, and
absolute, almighty God. There is a sense in which
we should take our shoes off our feet whenever we
use the name.[1]

While we may cringe and actually voice displeasure when we
hear someone taking God's name in vain, we would do well to examine our own heart attitude. Indifference and lack of respect due His
name from those who love Him may be just as heinous a sin.

Unfortunately, it is this latter problem that often plagues
Christianity. When believers have a low view of God, everything
focuses on meeting felt needs within the body of Christ. When the
church adopts such a perspective, it often offers people nothing
more than spiritual placebos. It centers on psychology, self-esteem,
entertainment, and a myriad of other diversions to attempt to meet
perceived and felt needs.

It is essential, however, that the church and each individual
believer in it understand they exist to bring glory to God. When
you know and glorify God, the needs of your life will be met: "The
fear of the LORD is the beginning of wisdom" (Prov. 9:10). But many
believers don't revere God; their very actions prove their irreverence.
Instead of trembling at God's Word, they twist His truths or sup-
plant them with worldly philosophies.

Christians actually need to be confronted by their real need—an
understanding of God's holiness and their own sinfulness—so they
can be usable to Him for His glory. When we have a right relationship

to God, every aspect of our lives will settle into its divinely ordained place. That does not mean we are to ignore people's problems—we are to be just as concerned about them as God is. But there must be a balance, and it begins with a high view of God. We must take God seriously and respect Him completely.

With that in mind, you can understand why prayer is ever and always, first and foremost, a recognition of God's majestic glory and our submission to it. All our petitions, all our needs, and all our problems are subject to Him. God is to have priority in every aspect of our lives, and certainly in our times of deepest communion with Him. Prayer is not to be a casual routine that gives passing homage to God; it is to be a profound experience that should open up great dimensions of reverence, awe, appreciation, honor, and adoration.

The Significance of God's Name

How appropriate then that the first petition in our Lord's pattern for prayer focuses on God: "hallowed be Your name" (Matt. 6:9). Commentator Arthur W. Pink said, "How clearly then is the fundamental duty of prayer set forth. Self and all its needs must be given a secondary place, and the Lord freely accorded the preeminence in our thoughts and supplications. This petition must take the precedence, for the glory of God's great name is the ultimate end of all things."[2] Even though He is our loving Father, who desires to meet our needs through His heavenly resources, our first petition is not to be for our benefit, but His. Thus "hallowed be Your name" is a warning against self-seeking prayer because it completely encompasses God's nature and man's response to it. Jesus wasn't reciting some nice words about

God. Instead, He opened a whole dimension of respect, reverence, glory, and worship for God.

The most familiar Hebrew name for God is Yahweh, and it first appears in Exodus 3:14, where God said, "I AM WHO I AM." The other familiar name for God is Adonai, which means the "Lord God." Because they considered God's name sacred, the Jews would not actually pronounce Yahweh. Eventually Old Testament Jews took the consonants from Yahweh and the vowels from Adonai to form Jehovah. While taking such great pains to honor the sacredness of God's name, they thought little of dishonoring His person or disobeying His Word, thus making a mockery of their effort.

By focusing our thoughts on God's name, our Lord is teaching us that God's name signifies much more than His titles; it represents all that He is—His character, plan, and will. Certainly the Jews should have understood that, because in Old Testament times, names stood for more than just titles.

A Character Reference

In Scripture, a person's name represented his character. While God characterized him as "a man after His own heart" (1 Sam. 13:14), David also developed a good reputation among the people: "The commanders of the Philistines went out to battle, and it happened as often as they went out, that David behaved himself more wisely than all the servants of Saul. So his name was highly esteemed" (18:30). The fact that his name was esteemed meant he himself was esteemed. When we say that someone has a good name, we mean there is something about his character worthy of our praise.

When Moses went up on Mount Sinai to receive the commandments for the second time, he "called upon the name of the LORD. Then the LORD passed by in front of him and proclaimed, 'The LORD, the LORD God, compassionate and gracious, slow to anger, and abounding in lovingkindness and truth; who keeps lovingkindness for thousands, who forgives iniquity, transgression and sin'" (Ex. 34:5–7). The name of God is the composite of all the characteristics listed in verses 6–7.

Our love and trust of God are not based on His names or titles, but on that reality behind those names: His character. David said, "Those who know Your name will put their trust in You, for You, O LORD, have not forsaken those who seek You" (Ps. 9:10). God's name is esteemed in His faithfulness.

In the typical form of Hebrew poetry, God's righteousness and His name are often typified as parallel, showing their equivalence. Thus David declared, "I will give thanks to the LORD according to His righteousness and will sing praise to the name of the LORD Most High" (Ps. 7:17). When the psalmist said, "Some boast in chariots and some in horses, but we will boast in the name of the LORD, our God" (20:7), he had much more in mind than God's title; he was referring to the fullness of God's person.

When Christ came into the world, people—especially the disciples—had the opportunity to see God's character in person. In His High Priestly Prayer, Jesus said to the Father, "I have manifested Your name to the men whom You gave Me" (John 17:6). He didn't need to tell them about God's name, but He did need to reveal God's character to them. John 1:14 tells how that was accomplished: "The Word became flesh, and dwelt among us, and we saw His glory, glory as of the only begotten from the Father, full of grace and truth." Christ manifested God to the disciples through His own righteous life. That's why he told Philip, "He who has seen Me has seen the Father" (John 14:9).

To apply the concept of hallowing God's name to your prayers, here is a sample you could use: "Our Father, who loves us and cares for us, and who has in heaven supplies to meet our every need; may Your person, Your identity, Your character, Your nature, Your attributes, Your reputation, Your very being itself be hallowed." To hallow God's name is not some glib phrase inserted into a prayer ritual; it is your opportunity to glorify Him by acknowledging the greatness and wonder of His character.

It's All in a Name

Each of the many Old Testament names and titles of God shows a different facet of His character and its expression in His will. He is called, for example, *Elohim,* "the Creator God"; *El Elyon,* "possessor of heaven and earth"; *JehovahJireh,* "the Lord will provide"; *JehovahNissi,* "the Lord our banner"; *JehovahRapha,* "the Lord that healeth"; *JehovahShalom,* "the Lord our peace"; *JehovahRaah,* "the Lord our Shepherd"; *JehovahTsidkenu,* "the Lord our righteousness"; *JehovahSabaoth,* "the Lord of hosts"; *JehovahShama,* "the Lord is present and near"; and *JehovahMaqodeshkim,* which means "the Lord sanctifieth thee." All those names speak of God's attributes. Thus they tell us not only who He is but also what He is like.

Jesus Himself provides the clearest teaching about what God's name means: His very name, *Jesus Christ,* is God's greatest name, and it encompasses His role as Lord, Savior, and King. As Jesus Christ,

God drew to Himself many other names, including: the Bread of Life (John 6:35), the Living Water (John 4:10), the Way, the Truth, and the Life (John 14:6), the Resurrection (John 11:25), the Good Shepherd (John 10:11), the Branch (Isa. 4:2), the Bright Morning Star (Rev. 22:16), the Lamb of God (John 1:29), and many more. One Old Testament passage in particular lists several names for Him, each one a designation of His nature: "Wonderful Counselor, Mighty God, Eternal Father, Prince of Peace" (Isa. 9:6). Jesus' life was the perfect manifestation of God's name.

Holy Is His Name

Having looked at the significance of God's name, we need to turn our attention to the meaning of the word *hallow*. It is actually an archaic English word used to translate a form of the Greek word *hagiazō*, which means "to make holy." Words from the same Greek root are translated *holy, saint, sanctify,* and *sanctification.*

God commands His people to be holy (1 Peter 1:16), but only God Himself is actually holy. To pray "hallowed be Your name" is to attribute to God the holiness that already is, and has always been, supremely and uniquely His. To hallow God's name is to revere, honor, glorify, and obey Him as the one and only completely perfect God. When we do, we remind ourselves of the important difference between us and Him. God lives in a different sphere than we do. He is holy and undefiled, but we are sinners. Only through His gracious provision of Jesus Christ and His payment for the penalty of our sin are we even able to approach Him. We agree with John Calvin, who said that God should have His own honor, of which He is so worthy, and that we should never think or speak of Him without the greatest veneration.[3]

Failure to Honor God

In spite of all the shallow trends that plague much of current Christianity, there is still nothing more disturbing than a failure to recognize the most central truth about God: He is holy. It is the only one of His attributes repeated three times in the heavenly realm (Isa. 6:3). Failure to give God the reverence and honor He so richly deserves can result in devastating consequences. The following narrative shows what can happen when even one of God's greatest servants doesn't treat Him with the respect due His name:

> Then the sons of Israel, the whole congregation, came to the wilderness of Zin in the first month; and the people stayed at Kadesh.... There was no water for the congregation, and they assembled themselves against Moses and Aaron. The people thus contended with Moses and spoke, saying, "If only we had perished when our brothers perished before the LORD! Why then have you brought the LORD's assembly into this wilderness, for us and our beasts to die here? Why have you made us come up from Egypt, to bring us in to this wretched place? It is not a place of grain or figs or vines or pomegranates, nor is there water to drink." Then Moses and Aaron came in from the presence of the assembly to the doorway of the tent of meeting, and fell on

their faces. Then the glory of the LORD appeared to them; and the LORD spoke to Moses, saying, "Take the rod; and you and your brother Aaron assemble the congregation and speak to the rock before their eyes, that it may yield its water. You shall thus bring forth water for them out of the rock and let the congregation and their beasts drink." So Moses took the rod from before the LORD, just as He had commanded him; and Moses and Aaron gathered the assembly before the rock. And he said to them, "Listen now, you rebels; shall we bring forth water for you out of this rock?" Then Moses lifted up his hand and struck the rock twice with his rod; and water came forth abundantly, and the congregation and their beasts drank. But the LORD said to Moses and Aaron, "Because you have not believed Me, to treat Me as holy in the sight of the sons of Israel, therefore you shall not bring this assembly into the land which I have given them." (Num. 20:1–12)

Moses dishonored God before the Israelites because he struck the rock, in direct disobedience to God. Moses' actions drew the attention of the people to himself, perhaps to make them think he had something to do with the miracle. But by stealing the glory from God and failing to honor Him, both Moses and Aaron were not allowed to enter the Promised Land.

The catalog of others who dishonored God is numerous. The following is only a small sampling:

- **Saul** did not submit himself to God, but in impatience and self-styled disobedience, he failed to follow all of God's instructions (1 Sam. 15:11), so God removed him from the throne.

- **Uzzah** failed to recognize the majesty of God's holiness by daring to defy God's instructions (Num. 4:15, 19–20). God struck him down for his irreverence (2 Sam. 6:7).

- **Uzziah** became proud, acted in a corrupt manner, was unfaithful to the Lord, and in an affront to God's holiness, entered the temple to burn incense. God struck him with leprosy (2 Chron. 26:16–23).

- **Ananias and Sapphira** lied to the Holy Spirit. By sinning against the holiness of God in such a way, they lost their lives within hours of their deceit (Acts 5:1–11).

- **The Corinthians** ate of the bread and drank from the cup in an unholy manner during the Lord's Supper (1 Cor. 11:27–30). As a result, many became sick, and some even died.

God does not always deal as immediately and directly in physical ways with those who fail to uphold His holy character. But there will always be some consequence. Here are a few of the main ones: It gives the enemy an opportunity to blaspheme God. That is what Nathan told David (2 Sam. 12:14; cf. Ezek. 20:39;

1 Tim. 5:14; 6:1). God's Word is dishonored (Titus 2:5). Sin can disqualify you from further service in the King's court. Saul is the classic illustration of that (1 Sam. 15:23). You can lose your life or well-being (Acts 5:5, 10). God may withhold spiritual blessings (Num. 20:1–12). God's anger is invoked (Isa. 5:25). God's Spirit is grieved (Isa. 63:10).

The Fear of the Lord Is Not an Option

The psalmist asked, "Who may dwell on Your holy hill?" (Ps. 15:1). The answer is simply, "He who walks with integrity, and works righteousness, and speaks truth in his heart" (v. 2). There is no greater need today than for believers once again to ascend the platform of fearing God.

A. W. Tozer said it well: "No religion has been greater than its idea of God." That gem has a corollary: No church is greater than its reverent awe of holy God. He is holy and demands recognition as such. Although most believers know that intellectually, I'm afraid very few realize what that means practically.

Clearly the fear of God is not optional: "Live in the fear of the LORD always" (Prov. 23:17); "fear Him who is able to destroy both soul and body in hell" (Matt. 10:28); "in all things obey … fearing the Lord" (Col. 3:22). Central to the book of Proverbs is the Hebrew word *yare*, which refers to fear and honor. Solomon used it eighteen times.

God has always called His people to have such a perspective of the awesomeness of His holiness:

- The fear of God pressed Manoah to expect instant death because he had seen God (Judg. 13:22).

- Upon seeing the magnitude of God's holiness, Job repented and retracted all that he had foolishly said (Job 42:5–6).

- Standing in the presence of God's holiness, Isaiah pronounced a curse on himself, "Woe is me, for I am ruined!" (Isa. 6:5).

- Habakkuk trembled at the voice of holy God (Hab. 3:16).

- The restored remnant feared the Lord when they heard His holy word spoken by the prophet Haggai (Hag. 1:12).

- During our Lord's earthly ministry, the disciples often came face-to-face with His power and holiness. On one occasion when they were crossing the Sea of Galilee, a storm appeared. Although they were afraid of the storm, they feared greatly (literally "feared a great fear") when Jesus calmed the storm (Mark 4:41). They became much more fearful of the presence and power of God than they were of the deadly storm. Stained by the sin of unbelief, Peter implored his sinless Lord to depart from him (Luke 5:8). John, James, and Peter fell on their faces and were exceedingly afraid when they heard the voice of God (Matt. 17:6).

- People in an unbelieving community begged Christ

to leave their region because they feared His holy power (Mark 5:17).

- The Jerusalem church was in deep awe of God's holiness (Acts 2:43; 5:5, 11), and throughout Judea, Galilee, and Samaria, the churches continued on in fear of the Lord (Acts 9:31).

- Beholding the magnificence of the glorified Christ, John fell in fear at His feet as a dead man (Rev. 1:17).

In each of those examples, God's presence produced the "anxiety of holiness." As I stated at the beginning of this chapter, that is an attitude largely missing in our method-oriented, pragmatic day. And it is especially missing in our prayers. To revive it, we must pursue holiness in the fear of God. That has always been God's desire for His people: "I am the LORD your God. Consecrate yourselves therefore, and be holy, for I am holy" (Lev. 11:44). Peter echoed that plea: "But like the Holy One who called you, be holy yourselves also in all your behavior; because it is written, 'You shall be holy, for I am holy'" (1 Peter 1:15–16; cf. Lev. 19:2). Today the challenge for Christ's church is this: "Let us cleanse ourselves from all defilement of flesh and spirit, perfecting holiness in the fear of God" (2 Cor. 7:1).

How to Hallow God's Name

Hallowing God's name, like every other manifestation of righteousness, begins in the heart. The apostle Peter said to "sanctify Christ as Lord in your hearts" (1 Peter 3:15). When we sanctify Christ in our hearts, we will also sanctify Him in our lives. Let's look at some practical ways you can do just that and also make sure God is hallowed in your prayer life.

Acknowledge God Exists

Hebrews 11:6 says, "He who comes to God must believe that He is." To the honest and open mind, God is self-evident. Philosopher Immanuel Kant had many strange ideas about God, but he was absolutely right when he said, "The moral law within us and the starry heavens above us" drive us to God.[4] But that is not enough—you can believe God exists and still not hallow His name.

Know the Truth about God

Many people claim they believe in God, but they don't hallow His name because they don't have true knowledge of who He is. Discovering and believing truth about God demonstrates reverence for Him; willing ignorance or believing wrong doctrine demonstrates irreverence.

Some people think that taking God's name in vain is swearing or cursing only, but that is not the case. You can take the name of the Lord in vain every time you think a thought about God that's not true, or when you doubt Him, disbelieve Him, and question Him. The early church father Origen said in his rebuttal to the Greek philosopher Celsus that the man who brings into his concept of God ideas that have no place there takes the name of the Lord God in vain.[5]

Some claim that God is harsh and vindictive, accusing Him of being unloving, of indiscriminately banishing people to an eternal hell—a national ally of Israel who slaughters other nations. Job fell into that same accusatory sin when he said, "You have become cruel to me" (Job 30:21). We cannot revere a God whose character and will we do not know or care about. Even when we know and revere Him, that is still not enough.

Be Aware of His Presence

As I stated in the first chapter, if we are to be faithful believers, we must live every day of our lives in a continual state of God consciousness. Spasmodic reflection does not hallow God's name. I am sure He is on the thoughts of many right after a Sunday morning worship service, but what about later that day and throughout the week? Those are the times you must consciously draw Him into every daily thought, word, and activity if you would truly hallow God's name. That was David's focus: "I have set the LORD continually before me" (Ps. 16:8). But that is still not enough to truly hallow God's name.

Live in Obedience

Our Father's name is most hallowed when we behave in conformity to His will. For Christians to live in disobedience to God is the ultimate in taking His name in vain, claiming as Lord someone we're not even willing to follow. Jesus warned, "Not everyone who says to Me, 'Lord, Lord,' will enter the kingdom of heaven, but he who does the will of My Father who is in heaven will enter" (Matt. 7:21).

When we disobey God, we diminish our capacity to revere His name and be a vehicle for manifesting His holiness. We will succeed in hallowing God's name, however, when we eat, drink, and do everything else to His glory (1 Cor. 10:31). We also honor His name when we attract others to Him because of our commitment. We are to "let [our] light shine before men in such a way that they may see [our] good works, and glorify [our] Father who is in heaven" (Matt. 5:16).

When you have the right thoughts about God and live righteously, you will hallow His name. Psalm 34:3 sums up the teaching of this phrase with this exhortation: "O magnify the LORD with me, and let us exalt His name together."

The next time you pray, I hope you see yourself entering the very throne room of God, a holy place, where He is to be honored. Don't be afraid when you enter that time of solitude with the God of heaven—just be sure you approach that time with the respect due His most holy name.

5

"YOUR KINGDOM COME"

In recent years, we have witnessed the rapid decline of more than 150 years of strong Christian biblical influence in this country. A few years ago someone suggested that we were living in post-Christian America. Although it struggles to deserve a nominal Christian label, today it is more like sub-Christian America. People attend religious services and say they believe in God, but at best they adhere to a practical atheism and situational morality. Whatever vestiges of Christian religion still remain in our culture have become weak and compromising, if not cultic and apostate.

Our nation now affirms, through its legislative bodies and courts, a distinctively anti-Christian agenda. Anything singularly Christian has been virtually swept away under the aegis of equal rights and moral freedom. The divine standards and biblical morality that our nation once embraced are assaulted constantly. Moral freedom now reigns. Materialism and the breakdown of the family are epidemic.

Abortions, sexual evils, drugs, and crime are rampant. And our leaders are at a loss to know what to do because there are no standards left to provide controls for these problems.

For those of us who remember the great revival of the '70s, the debauchery of modern times is especially saddening. But that sadness, if left unchecked, can lead to resentment—particularly toward those in control of the government, the media, and society who encourage an anti-Christian agenda.

What concerns me most, however, is the open hostility that resentment with our nation's leadership often fosters. When that attitude merges with the perspective that Christians ought to impact the culture by legislating morality, the church is severely diverted from its main purpose. Although changing our society by calling it back to a safer morality is a noble goal, this has never been Christ's goal for His church.

The church has but one mission in this world: to lead people destined to spend eternity in hell to a saving knowledge of Jesus Christ and an eternity in heaven. If people die in a communist government or a democracy, under a tyrant or a benevolent dictator, believing homosexuality is right or wrong, or believing abortion is a woman's fundamental right to choose or simply mass murder, that has no bearing on where they will spend eternity. If they never knew Christ and never embraced Him as their Lord and Savior, they will spend eternity in hell.

"My kingdom is not of this world," Jesus told Pilate. "If My kingdom were of this world, then My servants would be fighting so that I would not be handed over to the Jews" (John 18:36). No human kingdom or society can ever merge with God's kingdom, even partially. Sinful man cannot be a part of the divine reign. That's why we can never advance God's kingdom by trying to improve the morals of our society.

Good and noble causes may be worthy of support, but they have no impact in helping to usher in the earthly kingdom of Jesus Christ. At best they can only retard the corruption that will always and inevitably characterize human societies and kingdoms.

America has but one destiny: to go the way of all the other nations. No human kingdom will endure forever because built into it are the sinful seeds of its own destruction: "Righteousness exalts a nation, but sin is a disgrace to any people" (Prov. 14:34); "In the generations gone by He permitted all the nations to go their own ways" (Acts 14:16).

While all the kingdoms of the world, including America, rise and fall, the gates of hell will never prevail against God's kingdom (Matt. 16:18). You may be frustrated by our nation's immoral agenda and its animosity toward God, but you can be confident that even now Christ is building His church. One day the Lord will return to establish His own perfect kingdom. That's when we will finally realize what we have so anxiously longed for and what the disciples of Christ in the first century desired: to see Christ rule on the earth and the people of the world bow to Him.

Eighteenth-century hymn writer Frances Havergal beautifully captured that sentiment in these words to Christ in "His Coming to Glory":

Oh, the joy to see Thee reigning,
Thee, my own beloved Lord!

Every tongue Thy name confessing,
Worship, honor, glory, blessing
Brought to Thee with glad accord;
Thee, my Master and my Friend,
Vindicated and enthroned;
Unto earth's remotest end
Glorified, adored, and owned.

The Promise of God

The one who has the right to rule and reign is none other than the King Himself, the King of Kings and Lord of Lords, Jesus Christ. Psalm 2:6–8 says of Him, "I have installed My King upon Zion, My holy mountain. I will surely tell of the decree of the LORD: He said to Me, 'You are My Son, today I have begotten You. Ask of Me, and I will surely give the nations as Your inheritance, and the very ends of the earth as Your possession.'" Isaiah 9:6 says, "The government will rest on His shoulders." Jesus Christ is the One who fulfilled the promise of a coming King. He is the *Messiah*—the "anointed one." He is the hope of Israel, the hope of the church, and the hope of the world.

In one of his dreams, Daniel saw a statue representing the kingdoms of the world smashed to pieces by a flying stone, which represents Christ (Dan. 2:34–35). Then the stone filled the whole earth. The symbolism is clear: Christ ultimately crushes the kingdoms of men and establishes His own.

Christ is inseparable from His kingdom. The holy purpose of God is to exalt Christ in the consummation of history when the

Son rules and reigns in His kingdom. The Jewish Talmud is right in saying that the prayer in which there is no mention of the kingdom of God is not a prayer at all (*Berakoth* 21a).

Our New Priority

Our greatest desire as believers should be to see the Lord reigning as King in His kingdom, having the honor and authority that have always been His but that He has not yet come to claim. That leads to the second petition in our pattern of prayer from Matthew 6:10. To pray "Your kingdom come" is to pray for God's program to be fulfilled—for Christ to come and reign.

When you sincerely believe and genuinely confess Christ as Lord, you are confirming that the direction of your life is aimed at His exaltation. Your own causes are valid only insofar as they agree with the eternal causes of God revealed in Christ. When I pray, "Your kingdom come," I am saying to God's Holy Spirit, "Spirit of Christ within me, take control and do what You will for Your glory." A true child of God won't be preoccupied with his own plans and desires but with the determinate program of God, revealed in the person of Jesus Christ.

Dealing with Self

In spite of our desire to be preoccupied with God's kingdom, our prayers are usually self-centered. We focus on our needs, our plans, and our aspirations. We are often like tiny infants, who know no world but that of their own feelings and wants. Our lives are an unending struggle against our old sinful habits, with their constant and unrelenting focus on self.

Even problems and issues others face can cloud our supreme concern for God's kingdom. It is our responsibility to pray for our families, pastors, missionaries, national and other leaders, and many other people and things. But in every case, our prayers should be for God to accomplish His will in and through those people—that they would think, speak, and act in accordance with His will.

The kingdom must be at the heart of our prayers. Before we go bursting into His presence with all our petitions, we need to stop long enough to consider His causes and His kingdom. We must affirm our yearning that He be glorified in His purposes.

Dealing with Satan

As soon as we desire to live a holy life for Christ, we run into a massive conflict. The greatest opposition to Christ's kingdom, and the greatest opposition to Christian living, is the kingdom of this present world, which Satan rules. The next time you begin to resent the latest victory for the ungodly agenda in our country, consider the source. The essence of Satan's kingdom has always been opposition to God's kingdom and God's people. Satan will challenge every believer's effort to live a holy and God-honoring life.

A Kingdom Not of This World

The Greek word translated "kingdom" (*basileia*) does not primarily refer to a geographical territory but to sovereignty and dominion. Therefore when we pray, "Your kingdom come," we are praying for God's rule on earth to begin as Christ assumes His rightful place as ruler of the earth. "Come" translates the aorist active imperative form of *erchomai*, indicating a sudden, instantaneous coming (cf. Matt. 24:27). It is the coming of His millennial kingdom (Rev. 20:4) we are to pray for.

It Belongs to God

The kingdom we are praying for is unique because it doesn't belong to any earthly monarch; it belongs to "our Father who is in heaven" (Matt. 6:9). As believers, we are no longer of this world (John 17:14). Our primary interest has been translated out of this world, and our real citizenship is now in heaven (Phil. 3:20). We are but sojourners and pilgrims (1 Peter 1:17), waiting to enter a city whose builder and maker is God (Heb. 11:10).

God's kingdom is not at all like the manmade kingdoms of this world. Egypt, Assyria, Babylon, MedoPersia, Greece, and Rome are no longer world powers—their time in the spotlight was brief. Alexander the Great had one of the greatest empires in the entire history of the world, but it too is gone. All the once-great civilizations are extinct.

What Daniel said in reference to the end of the Babylonian empire could refer to all the nations of the world: "God has numbered your kingdom and put an end to it.... You have been weighed on the scales and found deficient.... Your kingdom has been divided and given over to the Medes and Persians" (Dan. 5:26–28). Earthly kingdoms go the way of all flesh—the degenerating power of sin causes inevitable decay and destruction.

But the kingdom of God is bigger than any nation. Our Lord said to "seek first His kingdom and His righteousness, and all these things will be added to you" (Matt. 6:33). He will take care of all our needs—clothing, shelter, and food—when we seek His kingdom. So we should pray, "Lord, do whatever advances Your kingdom and brings about Your reign."

Christ Is the Ruler

The kingdom of God, or of heaven, was the heart of Jesus' message. It is the gospel—the Good News of the kingdom of our Lord and of His Christ. Wherever He went, Jesus preached the message of salvation. He even said, "I must preach the kingdom … for I was sent for this purpose" (Luke 4:43). The reign of Christ is nothing less than the apex of human history. Jesus spent three years with the disciples teaching them about the kingdom. After He died and rose again, He appeared to them over a period of forty days, giving them commandments pertaining to the kingdom of God (Acts 1:2–3).

Jesus spoke of God's kingdom in three ways: past, present, and future. It is past in that it embodied Abraham, Isaac, and Jacob (Matt. 8:11). It was present during Jesus' own earthly ministry in that He was the true King living in the midst of the people (Luke 17:21). But the particular focus of our prayers is on the kingdom that is yet to come.

As we saw earlier, Jesus characterized the kingdom as not of this world (John 18:36). But what kind of kingdom is it, and how can it be here yet still be in the future? We need to examine two aspects of the kingdom: It is both universal and earthly.

The Universal Aspect

God is the ruler of the universe. He created it, He controls it, and He holds it together. James Orr commented, "There is therefore recognized in Scripture … a natural and universal kingdom or dominion of God embracing all objects, persons, and events, all doings of individuals and nations, all operations and changes of nature and history, absolutely without exception."[1] God's is an "everlasting kingdom" (Ps. 145:13), and even now "His sovereignty rules over all" (103:19). God is the universal King, and He mediates His rulership through His Son, by whom He made the worlds, and of whom it is said, "He is before all things, and in Him all things hold together" (Col. 1:17).

The Earthly Aspect

When Jesus said, "Your kingdom come" in His model prayer, He was saying in effect, "May the universal kingdom established in heaven come to earth." Notice the last words in Matthew 6:10: "on earth as it is in heaven." That is typical Hebrew parallelism, and it can relate to the first three petitions in the Disciples' Prayer. We could say, "Hallowed be Your name on earth as it is in heaven. Your kingdom come on earth as it is in heaven. Your will be done on earth as it is in heaven."

Since God is not now ruling on earth as He rules in heaven, we are to pray for the divine *earthly* kingdom to come—for Christ to return and establish His earthly kingdom, put down sin, and enforce obedience to God's will. The Lord will then rule "with a rod of iron" (Rev. 2:27). After a thousand years His earthly kingdom will merge into His eternal kingdom, and there will be no distinction between His rule on earth and His rule in heaven.

Bringing God's Kingdom to Earth

The best way to translate the phrase *Your kingdom come* is: "Let Your kingdom come now." What features lead to the consummation of His rule on earth?

The Conversion of Unbelievers

In a present and limited, but real and miraculous, way, God's kingdom is coming to earth each time a new soul is brought into the kingdom. Thus "Your kingdom come" is an evangelistic prayer.

Presently Christ's kingdom exists on earth internally in the hearts and minds of believers. We ought to pray for God's kingdom to increase. Praying for the kingdom to come, in this sense, is praying for the salvation of souls. The kingdom is the sphere of salvation entered by repentance and faith in Jesus Christ.

Conversion to God's kingdom begins with an invitation. In Matthew 22, Jesus likened the kingdom of heaven to a man hosting a large wedding banquet. The man sent out invitations to the guests. When those who were invited initially refused to come, the man said, "Go therefore to the main highways, and as many as you find there, invite to the wedding feast" (v. 9). Christ's invitation is worldwide.

This invitation into the kingdom of God demands repentance. Jesus said, "Repent, for the kingdom of heaven is at hand" (Matt. 4:17; cf. Mark 1:14–15). And that requires a willing response on the part of the hearer. Jesus once told a scribe, "You are not far from the kingdom of God" (Mark 12:34). While he had knowledge about salvation, he had not made any conscious choice to receive it. Knowledge of the kingdom goes only so far. If people desire Christ to rule in their hearts and minds, they must respond to what they know.

Jesus said, "Seek first His kingdom and His righteousness" (Matt. 6:33). People who truly desire to know Christ will respond to the invitation by seeking Christ with all their hearts. Luke 16:16

says, "The Law and the Prophets were proclaimed until John; since that time the gospel of the kingdom of God has been preached, and everyone is forcing his way into it." The Greek word translated "forcing" means "to enter violently." When a person with a right heart sees the value of God's kingdom, he rushes to grasp it. The kingdom of heaven is of such infinite value that it is like "a treasure hidden in the field" or a "pearl of great value," which a person sells all his possessions to buy (Matt. 13:44–46).

The Commitment of Believers

The desire of those already converted should be to allow the Lord to rule in their lives now, just as He rules in heaven. We frequently come to crossroads in our lives where we have to choose between doing God's will or our own. That's when we need to affirm our commitment to God's causes. Since Christ is Lord, we must submit to His lordship. In Romans 14:17, the apostle Paul said, "The kingdom of God is not eating and drinking, but righteousness and peace and joy in the Holy Spirit." When you commit yourself to the virtues the Spirit wants to produce in your life, you will pray that your life will honor and glorify your Father in heaven.

The Commencement of Christ's Earthly Rule

One day the heavens will split open and Jesus will descend onto the Mount of Olives to establish His kingdom (Zech. 14:4). He will reign for a thousand years (Rev. 20:4) and rule with a rod of iron (Rev. 19:15). At that time the prayer "Your kingdom come" will be answered. Christ will reign in righteousness, justice, truth, and peace. He will rule on the earth on the throne of David in the city of Jerusalem and will set right the curses that have plagued this earth. Like Peter, I look for and seek to hasten the day when He comes. And I say with the apostle John, "Come, Lord Jesus" (Rev. 22:20). I hope that will be your request every time you pray.

6

"YOUR WILL BE DONE"

One of the dilemmas Christians have debated for centuries is whether God accomplishes His will regardless if we pray or don't pray. When we pray sincerely and persistently as Christ has taught us—can our will override God's? When we don't pray, does His will fail? The plain fact is none of us can comprehend precisely how prayer functions in the infinite mind and plan of God. What seems like a hopeless mystery to us is no problem to God. But that doesn't mean theologians have not attempted to solve this dilemma.

Two basic doctrinal views have been offered to bring understanding to this question. One view emphasizes God's sovereignty and in its extreme application holds that God will work according to His perfect will regardless of how people pray or even whether they pray. Thus prayer is nothing more than tuning in to God's will. At the opposite extreme is the view that maintains God's actions pertaining to us are determined largely by our prayers. Our persistent pleading will make

God do for us what He wouldn't otherwise do. Pastor and author
James Montgomery Boice related the following humorous story about
how this paradox confounds even our greatest spiritual leaders:

> At one point in the course of their very influential
> ministries George Whitefield, the Calvinist evange-
> list, and John Wesley, the Arminian evangelist, were
> preaching together in the daytime and rooming
> together in the same boarding house each night. One
> evening after a particularly strenuous day the two of
> them returned to the boarding house exhausted and
> prepared for bed. When they were ready each knelt
> beside the bed to pray. Whitefield, the Calvinist,
> prayed like this, "Lord, we thank Thee for all those
> with whom we spoke today, and we rejoice that their
> lives and destinies are entirely in Thy hand. Honor
> our efforts according to Thy perfect will. Amen." He
> rose from his knees and got into bed. Wesley, who
> had hardly gotten past the invocation of his prayer
> in this length of time, looked up from his side of
> the bed and said, "Mr. Whitefield, is this where your
> Calvinism leads you?" Then he put his head down
> and went on praying. Whitefield stayed in bed and
> went to sleep. About two hours later Whitefield woke
> up, and there was Wesley still on his knees beside the
> bed. So Whitefield got up and went around the bed
> to where Wesley was kneeling. When he got there he
> found Wesley asleep. He shook him by the shoulder

and said to him, "Mr. Wesley, is this where your Arminianism leads you?"[1]

Like Whitefield and Wesley, we cannot begin to fathom the divine working that makes prayer effective. The Bible is unequivocal about God's absolute sovereignty, yet within His sovereignty, He commands us to exercise our responsible wills in certain areas, including beseeching Him in prayer. If God did not act in response to prayer, Jesus' teaching about prayer would be futile and meaningless and all commands to pray pointless. Our task is not to solve the dilemma of how God's sovereignty works with human responsibility but to believe and act on what God commands us about prayer.

To pray for God's will to be accomplished is the subject of our Lord's third petition in His pattern for prayer. After asking for God's name to be hallowed and His kingdom to come, Jesus said we are to pray, "Your will be done, on earth as it is in heaven" (Matt. 6:10). When we pray, we are to pray in accord with God's will. His will is to become our will. We are also praying for His will to prevail all over the earth, just as it does in heaven.

David prayed with the attitude of the third petition when he said, "I delight to do Your will, O my God" (Ps. 40:8). That was Christ's attitude as well: "My food is to do the will of Him who sent Me" (John 4:34; cf. Matt. 12:50; John 6:38).

Is God's Will Inevitable?

Unfortunately many people, including believers, don't have this same attitude toward the third petition of the Disciples' Prayer.

Bitter Resentment

Some professed believers resent what they see as the imposition of God's will—a divine dictator working out His sovereign, selfish will on His people. They pray out of a sense of compulsion, believing they cannot escape from the inevitable. Commentator William Barclay said:

> A man may say, "Thy will be done," in a tone of defeated resignation. He may say it, not because he wishes to say it, but because he has accepted the fact that he cannot possibly say anything else; he may say it because he has accepted the fact that God is too strong for him, and that it is useless to batter his head against the walls of the universe.[2]

Eleventh-century Persian poet Omar Khayyám had a similar perspective of God. In the *Rubáiyát,* a collection of his four-lined epigrams, he wrote:

> *But helpless Pieces of the Game He plays*
> *Upon this Checkerboard of Nights and Days;*
> *Hither and thither moves, and checks, and slays,*
> *And one by one back in the Closet lays.*
>
> *The Ball no question makes of Ayes and Noes,*
> *But Here or There as strikes the Player goes;*
> *And He that tossed you down into the Field,*
> *He knows about it all—He knows—He knows! (vv. 69–70)*

This Persian poet viewed God as a checker player with total power over the playing pieces, moving them at His whim and putting them in the closet when He was done. The poet also saw God as a polo player with a mallet and man as the ball that has absolutely no choice about how it is hit or where it goes. But such a perspective reflects a lack of knowledge about how God truly interacts with His people.

Passive Resignation

Other believers, however, don't resent God's will. They view Him as their loving, caring Father who has only their best in mind. Yet they also are resigned to His will as the inevitable, unchangeable, and irresistible force in their lives, thus they think their prayers will not make a difference. They pray for His will to be done only because He has commanded them to do so. But that's certainly not a prayer of faith; it's more like a prayer of capitulation. Believers who pray that way accept God's will with a defeatist attitude.

Too many believers have weak prayer lives because they don't believe their prayers accomplish anything. They petition the Lord for something and then forget about it, acting as if they knew in advance that God wouldn't be at all compelled to grant what they requested. Even in the early days of the church, when faith generally was strong and vital, prayer could be passive and unexpectant. When the apostle Peter was imprisoned in Jerusalem, a group of concerned believers met at the house of Mary, John Mark's mother, to pray for his release (Acts 12:12). As they were doing so, an angel of the Lord miraculously delivered Peter from his chains (vv. 7–10). While the believers were still praying, Peter arrived at the house and knocked on the door. A servant girl named Rhoda answered the door, and upon recognizing Peter's voice, she turned around and rushed to tell the others before letting Peter in (vv. 13–14). The others did not believe her, however, until they finally let Peter in. Then "they saw him and were amazed" (v. 16). They apparently had been praying for what they did not really believe would happen.

Prayer is not a vain duty to be performed for the sake of obedience only. That may seem like a good motive, but its effect is no different from the hypocritical Pharisees who prayed for show. We must pray in faith, believing that our prayers do make a difference to God. To guard against such passive and unspiritual resignation, Jesus told the disciples the parable of the importunate widow "to show that at all times they ought to pray and not to lose heart" (Luke 18:1).

Is God's Will Alive and Well on Earth?

Asking "Your will be done on earth" indicates that God's will is not always done on earth. That is also true of some other elements of this prayer. We pray "Hallowed be Your name," yet God's name is infrequently hallowed here. We ask for His kingdom to come, yet there are many who reject His reign. Thus His will is not inevitable. In fact, lack of faithful prayer inhibits God's will because in His wise and gracious plan, prayer is essential to the proper working of His will on earth.

The Impact of Sin

God is sovereign, but He is not independently deterministic. Too many believers look at God's sovereignty in a fatalistic way, thinking that whatever will be will be. They view every tragedy as coming from God's hand, whether it's personal, such as a loved one's death or illness, or universal, as in an earthquake or flood. But such an attitude destroys faithful prayer and faithful obedience. That is not a high view of God's sovereignty but a destructive and unbiblical view of it.

The entire course of events, and circumstances, is ordained by God, and that includes allowing the cause of all life's tragedies—sin. To see God as ultimately sovereign, we must agree that He meant for sin to happen. He planned for it—it could not have caught Him by surprise and spoiled His original program. Thus evil and all its consequences were included in God's eternal decree before the foundation of the world.

Yet we cannot consider God as the author or originator of sin. The apostle John said, "God is Light, and in Him there is no darkness at all" (1 John 1:5; cf. James 1:13). God did not authorize sin; neither does He condone or approve of it. He could never be the cause or agent of sin. He only permits evil agents to do their deeds, then overrules the evil for His own wise and holy ends. Certainly it is not God's will that people die, so He sent Christ to earth to destroy death. It is not His will that people go to hell, so He sent His Son to take the penalty of sin on Himself that men might escape hell. The apostle Peter said, "The Lord is not slow about His promise, as some count slowness, but is patient toward you, not wishing for any to perish but for all to come to repentance" (2 Peter 3:9). That sin exists on earth and causes such horrible consequences is not evidence of God's desire to see sin abound but of His patience in allowing more opportunity for people to turn to Him for salvation. Thus we can determine that God's purposes in permitting evil are always good.[3]

A tension will always exist between God's sovereignty and man's will; therefore, we should not try to resolve it by modifying what He says about either reality. God is sovereign, but He gives us choices. And it is in His sovereignty that He commands us to pray, "Your will be done, on earth as it is in heaven" (Matt. 6:10).

Righteous Rebellion

In the first chapter we examined Jesus' parable of the widow and the unjust judge (Luke 18:1–8). She certainly was not willing to accept her circumstances as they were, but persisted in pleading with the judge to deal with her problem. We need to possess that same perspective when praying for God's will to be done on earth. Theologian David Wells said, "To come to an acceptance of life 'as it is,' to accept it on its own terms—which means acknowledging the inevitability of the way it works—is to surrender a Christian view of God."[4]

A part of the right understanding of and attitude toward God's will is what might be called a sense of righteous rebellion. To be dedicated to God's will necessitates being opposed to Satan's. To pray "Your will be done, on earth as it is in heaven" is to rebel against the notion that sin is normal and inevitable and therefore should be tolerated. When you are wholly committed to seeing God's will done on earth, you will rebel against the world system of ungodliness. You will renounce all things that dishonor and reject Christ. And you will also confront the disobedience of believers. Impotence in prayer leads us, however unwillingly, to strike a truce with evil. When you accept what is, you abandon a Christian view of God and His plan for redemptive history.

Jesus knew in advance what would happen to Him, but He did not accept each situation as inevitable or irresistible. He preached and acted against sin. When His Father's house was profaned, "He made a scourge of cords, and drove them all out of the temple, with the sheep and the oxen; and He poured out the coins of the money changers, and overturned their tables; and to those who were selling the doves He said, 'Take these things away; stop making My Father's house a place of business'" (John 2:15–16; cf. Matt. 21:12–13).

To pray for God's will to be done on earth is to rebel against the idea, promulgated even among some evangelicals, that virtually every wicked, corrupt thing we do or is done to us is somehow God's holy will and should be accepted from His hand with thanksgiving. But nothing wicked or sinful ever comes from the hand of God, only from the hand of Satan. When we pray for righteousness, we pray against wickedness.

At this point, I must add a word of caution lest you take this idea of rebellion against the evil in our world too far.

While we should react negatively against evil and entreat God to accomplish His will here, we should not attempt to carry out God's will for Him. As we noted in chapter 5, it is not our responsibility, neither should it be our goal, to change the culture by trying to establish God's kingdom on earth. Neither are we to rid our culture of its evil practices by using civil disobedience to rebel against it. Such rebellion is disobedience to God and His Word (Rom. 13:1–5; 1 Peter 2:13–17). Instead, let your rebellion be manifested in your prayers and those activities that are righteous and allowable under the law.

To pray for God's will to be done is to pray for Satan's will to be undone. It is to cry with David, "Let God arise, let His enemies be scattered, and let those who hate Him flee before Him" (Ps. 68:1). And we plead with the saints under God's altar, "How long, O Lord, holy and true, will You refrain from judging and avenging our blood on those who dwell on the earth?" (Rev. 6:10).

I wish that was the perspective of every believer. What has happened to our passion for what is right? God loves heroic faith—He wants us to storm His throne.

Is God's Will Your Will?

Unfortunately, our own will is often the problem in seeking His will. Because we live in a culture that prides itself on ease and comfort, we desire a piece of that big pie. As a result, we tend to perceive prayer as important only for making a difference in our circumstances rather than for the difference it can make in us and for God's glory. Thus when God doesn't answer our prayers as we wish right away, we lose the passion necessary to persevere in intercession.

If you want to have that passion in your prayers, you need to realize that the real benefit of prayer is not the changes God may make in your circumstances but the changes He will make in you and in your perception of them. When He draws you into conformity to His blessed person and will, your circumstances, no matter how insurmountable they may have appeared at first, will no longer be your priority. That's because your attitude about them will be different.

When your prayers are rooted in your faith in God—when you believe He will hear and answer your prayers—you are praying with the right attitude and perspective. The greatest hindrance to prayer is not lack of technique, lack of biblical knowledge, or even lack of enthusiasm for the Lord's work, but lack of faith. We simply do not pray with the expectation that our prayers will make a difference in our lives, in the church, or in the world.

The Specifics of His Will

To help you understand more about this critical issue, we need to examine three distinct aspects of God's will as He reveals it to us in His Word.

God's Comprehensive Will

This refers to God's will of purpose—His vast, all-inclusive, tolerating will expressed in the unfolding of His sovereign plan in the entire universe, including heaven, hell, and earth. This aspect of God's will allows sin to run its course and Satan to have his way for a season. But in His appointed time, sin's course and Satan's way will end exactly according to God's plan and foreknowledge.

Isaiah wrote about God's ultimate will, saying, "The LORD of hosts has sworn saying, 'Surely, just as I have intended so it has happened, and just as I have planned so it will stand.... This is the plan devised against the whole earth; and this is the hand that is stretched out against all the nations. For the LORD of hosts has planned, and who can frustrate it?'" (Isa. 14:24, 26–27). Whatever God purposes to do will come to pass, and no one can hinder that plan.

"We know that God causes all things to work together for good to those who love God, to those who are called according to His purpose" (Rom. 8:28). Although God does not will evil, He takes the things that happen in history and in our lives and puts them together for good. And of course His greatest plan is the salvation of His people: "We have obtained an inheritance, having been predestined according to His purpose who works all things after the counsel of His will" (Eph. 1:11). God's great purpose is for a redeemed people, for a unified church, a body of saints for eternity.

How do we pray in accord with God's comprehensive will? By joyously joining in affirming and awaiting the accomplishment of His divine plans. Although we know that someday Christ will complete His church out of this world to be with Him just as God planned, we are to pray in anticipation of that great hour and for God to hasten the coming of it.

God's Compassionate Will

This aspect of God's will refers to His heart's desire, which is within the scope of His comprehensive will and completely consistent with it, although it is more specific and focused. Unlike God's comprehensive will, however, His desires are not always fulfilled. In fact, our present age attests that Satan's desires are realized more often than God's.

Jesus desired Jerusalem's salvation, and He prayed, preached, healed, and ministered to that end: "O Jerusalem, Jerusalem.... I wanted to gather your children together, just as a hen gathers her brood under her wings, and you would not have it!" (Luke 13:34). But what was the typical response to Jesus? Few believed Him; most rejected Him; and some even crucified Him. That Jesus said "You are unwilling to come to Me so that you may have life" (John 5:40) is a sad commentary on the choice of unbelief and the rejection of His offer of abundant life.

God, our Savior, "desires all men to be saved and to come to the knowledge of the truth" (1 Tim. 2:4). He does not wish for "any to perish but for all to come to repentance" (2 Peter 3:9). Unfortunately, that desire is not fulfilled in the lives of the majority of people. Instead they reject Christ, and the most the Lord will do for them is weep (Jer. 13:17).

God's Commanding Will

This aspect of His will relates directly to His children, because only they have the capacity to obey. God's ardent desire is that we who are His children obey Him completely and immediately with willing hearts. About our obedience Paul wrote:

> Do you not know that when you present yourselves
> to someone as slaves for obedience, you are slaves of
> the one whom you obey, either of sin resulting in
> death, or of obedience resulting in righteousness?
> But thanks be to God that though you were slaves
> of sin, you became obedient from the heart to that
> form of teaching to which you were committed,
> and having been freed from sin, you became slaves
> of righteousness. (Rom. 6:16–18)

Since we are God's servants, it is only natural that we obey His commanding will. As Peter said, "We must obey God rather than men" (Acts 5:29).

When you pray "Your will be done," you are praying for three things: the consummation of the world and the use of sin's consequences for God's eternal plan, the salvation of people who don't know God, and the obedience of every believer to God's commands.

When we studied the phrase "Your kingdom come," we learned the kingdom comes to earth in three ways: through the conversion of unbelievers; by the commitment of believers to live according to righteousness, peace, and joy in the Holy Spirit; and at the second coming of Christ when He establishes His earthly rule. I see a parallel between those three elements and the three aspects of God's will we just looked at. God's comprehensive will embraces the ultimate end of man's dominion on earth and the return of Christ to set up an eternal kingdom. His compassionate will embraces the conversion of unbelievers. And His commanding will demands commitment from His people.

Conforming to His Will

Our own pride is the major obstacle we must overcome before we can pray for God's will to be done in our lives. Pride caused Satan to rebel against God, and pride causes unbelievers to reject God and believers to disobey Him. To accept and pray for God's will in sincerity and faith, you must abandon your own will for the sake of God's. The apostle Paul told us how to do that:

> Therefore I urge you, brethren, by the mercies of God, to present your bodies a living and holy sacrifice, acceptable to God, which is your spiritual service of worship. And do not be conformed to this world, but be transformed by the renewing of your mind, so that you may prove what the will of God is, that which is good and acceptable and perfect. (Rom. 12:1–2)

Until you lay your life on God's altar as a living sacrifice—until your will is dead—God's will won't be manifest in your life.

When we pray in faith and in conformity to God's will, our prayer is a sanctifying grace that changes our lives dramatically. Thus prayer is a means of progressive sanctification. John Hannah, associate professor of historical theology at Dallas Theological Seminary, said, "The end of prayer is not so much tangible answers as a deepening life of dependency.... The call to prayer is a call primarily to love, submission, and obedience ... the avenue of sweet, intimate, and intense fellowship of the soul with the infinite Creator."[5] That's what being alone with God is all about. You'll realize power and passion in it when you are completely dependent on God and live in obedience to His will.

Author Philip Keller, while visiting in Pakistan, read Jeremiah 18:2, which says, "Arise and go down to the potter's house, and there I will announce My words to you." So he and a missionary went to a potter's house in that city. In his book *A Layman Looks at the Lord's Prayer*, he wrote:

> In sincerity and earnestness I asked the old master craftsman to show me every step in the creation of a masterpiece.... On his shelves were gleaming goblets, lovely vases, and exquisite bowls of breathtaking beauty.
>
> Then, crooking a bony finger toward me, he led the way to a small, dark, closed shed at the back of his shop. When he opened its rickety door, a repulsive, overpowering stench of decaying matter

engulfed me. For a moment I stepped back from the edge of the gaping dark pit in the floor of the shed. "This is where the work begins!" he said, kneeling down beside the black, nauseating hole. With his long, thin arm, he reached down into the darkness. His slim, skilled fingers felt around amid the lumpy clay, searching for a fragment of material exactly suited to his task.

"I add special kinds of grass to the mud," he remarked. "As it rots and decays, its organic content increases the colloidal quality of the clay. Then it sticks together better." Finally his knowing hands brought up a lump of dark mud from the horrible pit where the clay had been tramped and mixed for hours by his hard, bony feet.

With tremendous impact the first verses from Psalm 40 came to my heart. In a new and suddenly illuminating way I saw what the psalmist meant when he wrote long ago, "I waited patiently for the LORD, and he inclined unto me, and heard my cry. He brought me up also out of an horrible pit, out of the miry clay." As carefully as the potter selected his clay, so God used special care in choosing me....

The great slab of granite, carved from the rough rock of the high Hindu Kush mountains behind his home, whirled quietly. It was operated by a very crude, treadle-like device that was moved by his feet, very much like our antique sewing machines.

As the stone gathered momentum, I was taken in memory to Jeremiah 18:3. "Then I went down to the potter's house, and, behold, he wrought a work on the wheels."

But what stood out most before my mind at this point was the fact that beside the potter's stool, on either side of him, stood two basins of water. Not once did he touch the clay, now spinning swiftly at the center of the wheel, without first dipping his hands in the water. As he began to apply his delicate fingers and smooth palms to the mound of mud, it was always through the medium of the moisture of his hands. And it was fascinating to see how swiftly but surely the clay responded to the pressure applied to it through those moistened hands. Silently, smoothly, the form of a graceful goblet began to take shape beneath those hands. The water was the medium through which the master craftsman's will and wishes were being transmitted to the clay. His will actually was being done in earth.

For me this was a most moving demonstration of the simple, yet mysterious truth that my Father's will and wishes are expressed and transmitted to me through the water of His own Word....

Suddenly, as I watched, to my utter astonishment, I saw the stone stop. Why? I looked closely.

The potter removed a small particle of grit from the goblet…. Then just as suddenly the stone stopped again. He removed another hard object….

Suddenly he stopped the stone again. He pointed disconsolately to a deep, ragged gouge that cut and scarred the goblet's side. It was ruined beyond repair! In dismay he crushed it down beneath his hands….

"And the vessel that he made of clay was marred in the hand of the potter" (Jer. 18:4). Seldom had any lesson come home to me with such tremendous clarity and force. Why was this rare and beautiful masterpiece ruined in the master's hands? Because he had run into resistance. It was like a thunderclap of truth bursting about me!

Why is my Father's will—His intention to turn out truly beautiful people—brought to nought again and again? Why, despite His best efforts and endless patience with human beings, do they end up a disaster? Simply because they resist His will.

The sobering, searching, searing question I had to ask myself in the humble surroundings of that simple potter's shed was this: Am I going to be a piece of fine china or just a finger bowl? Is my life going to be a gorgeous goblet fit to hold the fine wine of God's very life from which others can drink and be refreshed? Or am I going to be just a crude finger bowl in which passersby will dabble their fingers briefly then pass on and forget about it? It was one of the most solemn moments in all of my spiritual experiences.

"Father, Thy will be done in earth [in clay], in me, as it is done in heaven."[6]

7

"GIVE US THIS DAY OUR DAILY BREAD"

Every child faces a life of dependence from the moment he is conceived. At the very start of his new life, he must look to his mother for nourishment in the womb. Once he is born, he is dependent on his parents for food, clothing, and shelter. He cannot provide any of those resources for himself. Unlike other earthly creatures, he can't even come to his mother; she has to come to him.

An infant is also incapable of caring for himself in terms of cleanliness. He is dependent on his mother and father to give him baths, clip his nails, comb his hair, and otherwise make him presentable. Once he becomes more mobile, the child is incapable of determining what is safe or harmful. Without his parents' guidance, he could fall down stairs, burn himself, eat something poisonous—any of which could permanently disable him or even kill him. No one would argue the necessity for round-the-clock care for infants.

In much the same way, Christians are like infants when it comes to total dependence on God. Just like infants, we are ultimately dependent on God for food, clothing, and shelter. Just as infants get dirty throughout the day, we live in a world of sin that pollutes our walk with Christ. While our Lord has paid the penalty for our sins past, present, and future, we still sin each day. We need to come to God confessing our sins so He will cleanse them and restore us to fellowship with Him. And just as infants desperately need the protection of their parents from harmful things, we are dependent on God to guard us from the circumstances in our lives that can hurt our spiritual walks.

Praying for Our Needs

Thus the second group of three petitions the Lord gives in His model prayer should not surprise us. After focusing our attention on our Heavenly Father, Jesus then showed us how to pray for our own special needs in this world: "Give us this day our daily bread. And forgive us our debts, as we also have forgiven our debtors. And do not lead us into temptation, but deliver us from evil" (Matt. 6:11–13). Although this second section of the prayer deals with man's need, it doesn't set God aside—He is also exalted here. The fact that God is the One who gives us our daily bread, forgives our debts, and keeps us from temptation is an expression of His power and grace. Thus He glorifies Himself by meeting those needs in our lives.

Of those three petitions, the Lord somewhat surprisingly told us to pray first for our physical needs, not our spiritual needs. Martyn Lloyd-Jones captures the essence of these three petitions:

Clearly the first thing that is necessary is that we must be enabled to continue our existence in this world. We are alive and we must be kept alive. The very fact of my existence and being are involved, so the first petition deals with the needs of our physical frame, and our Lord starts with that. He then goes on to deal with the need of cleansing from the defilement and guilt of sin; and, lastly, with the need for being kept from sin and its power. That is the true way to look at man's life. I am alive and I must be kept alive. But then I am conscious of guilt and unworthiness, and feel the need to be cleansed from that. Then I think of the future and realize that I need to be delivered from certain things that face me there.... The sum of it all is that ultimately there is nothing in the whole realm of Scripture which so plainly shows us our entire dependence upon God as does this prayer, and especially these three petitions. The only thing that really matters for us is that we know God as our Father. If we only knew God like this our problems would be solved already and we would realize our utter dependence upon Him and go to Him daily as children to their Father.[1]

As we examine these three petitions, I hope you will be instructed and motivated to go to Him daily and seek His provision for your needs.

Bread and Our Physical Needs

Praying for God to give them their daily bread may at first seem irrelevant to many believers in our country who don't have to speculate where their next meal is coming from.

Why should they ask God for what they already have, and in great abundance? What would be a completely understandable request by Christians in many African or Asian countries seems irrelevant to a well-fed American. So what application does this request have for believers who have abundance? Five key elements of the petition will provide the answer.

The Necessity of Life

The Greek word translated *bread* not only represents food but is also symbolic of all our physical needs. Theologian John Stott has observed that to Martin Luther, "everything necessary for the preservation of this life is bread, including food, a healthy body, good weather, house, home, wife, children, good government, and peace."[2] Please make note, however, that our Lord is referring to physical necessities, not luxuries; if God so chooses to bless any of us with luxuries, it is purely by His good grace.

It thrills me to know that the God who created the entire universe, who is the God of space, time, and eternity, who is infinitely holy and completely self-sufficient, should care about supplying my physical needs. Just as loving human fathers want to provide for the needs of their children, so God is concerned that we receive enough food to eat, clothes to wear, and a place to rest.

This petition is more than just a request for physical needs, however. Above all it recognizes and affirms that every good thing we have comes from the hand of God graciously (James 1:17). This is why it is as appropriate for those who have abundance as for those who suffer lack. Although we may not always be on the edge of hunger, we can always be thankful for everything God provides and avoid being presumptuous.

The Source of Our Provision

When all our needs are met and all is well in our lives, we tend to take credit for what we have, to feel that we carry our own loads. We work hard to earn the money we need to buy food and clothes, pay our rent or mortgage. But even the hardest-working individual owes all he earns to God's provision. Moses reminded Israel that God "is giving you power to make wealth" (Deut. 8:18).

Our life, breath, health, possessions, talents, and opportunities all originate from resources God has created and made available to man. Everything we have is from God: It is He who brings the rain to make things grow, causes the seasons to change, produces the minerals that make the soil fertile, provides the natural resources we use to propel ourselves around, and provides the animals and plants from which we make our clothing and food. Our daily bread—the necessities of physical life—are all from God.

In the garden of Eden, God provided for Adam and Eve even before He created them. After He made and blessed them, He said, "Behold, I have given you every plant yielding seed that is on the surface of all the earth, and every tree which has fruit yielding seed; it shall be food for you" (Gen. 1:29). Since that time He has continued to provide an abundance of food for mankind, in almost unlimited variety.

Yet the apostle Paul told us "The Spirit explicitly says that in later times some will fall away from the faith ... and advocate abstaining from foods which God has created to be gratefully shared in by those who believe and know the truth. For everything created by God is good, and nothing is to be rejected if it is received with gratitude; for it is sanctified by means of the word of God and prayer" (1 Tim. 4:1, 3–5). The Word of God sanctifies (sets apart from God) all food, and we sanctify it when we receive it with thankful prayer.

Do you have that attitude? Are you truly thankful to God for your food when you bow your head and say a prayer before a meal? For many of us, sadly, the prayer we offer to God before we eat is usually quick and indifferent—we're just making sure to do our duty. Such an attitude reveals the sin of indifference and ingratitude for God's gifts. Thomas Watson, a great Puritan with a heart for God, wrote:

> If all be a gift, see the odious ingratitude of men who sin against their giver! God feeds them, and they fight against him; he gives them bread, and they give him affronts. How unworthy is this! Should we not cry shame of him who had a friend always feeding him with money, and yet he should betray and injure him? Thus ungratefully do sinners deal with God; they not only forget his mercies, but abuse them. "When I had fed them to the full, they then committed adultery" (Jer. 5:7). Oh, how horrid is it to sin against a bountiful God!—to strike the hands that relieve us![3]

Never presuming on the grace of God's provisions and thanking Him for His daily kindness in meeting your physical needs fulfills the spirit of the petition, "Give us this day our daily bread." Realizing that God alone is the source of those provisions gives Him glory.

The Heart of the Petition

The heart of this petition is expressed in the word *give* because it recognizes the need of the petitioner. Even though God may have already provided the necessity, we ask Him for it in recognition of His past and present provision, as well as in trust for His future supply.

Jesus' instruction and our petitions in this model prayer are valid only because God has promised to provide for His people. We could not expect God to give what He has not promised—that would be presumptuous. But we can pray confidently because God has promised to supply abundantly.

In Psalm 37, David counseled us to trust in God's promise to provide for our needs.

> Trust in the LORD and do good; dwell in the land and cultivate faithfulness. Delight yourself in the LORD; and He will give you the desires of your heart.... Yet a little while and the wicked man will be no more.... But the humble will inherit the land and will delight themselves in abundant prosperity.... I have been young, and now I am old, yet I have not seen the righteous forsaken, or his descendants begging bread. (vv. 3–4, 10–11, 25)

One passage that refers to both the spiritual and physical aspects of our lives is 2 Corinthians 9. The context of this passage refers to believers' generosity concerning the needs of the saints: We are to give "not grudgingly or under compulsion, for God loves a cheerful giver" (v. 7). As we reveal our own desire to provide for the needs of others (v. 6), God "who supplies seed to the sower and bread for food will supply and multiply your seed for sowing and increase the harvest of your righteousness" (v. 10). When you invest in God's kingdom, He will provide not only spiritual fruit but also bread for food.

The Unrighteous Need Not Apply

God's physical provision is a biblical promise, but only to those who belong to Him—the "us" of Matthew 6:11. Notice that David is speaking to believers in Psalm 37: They "trust in the LORD" (v. 3), "delight ... in the LORD" (v. 4), "commit [their] way to the LORD" (v. 5), and "rest in the LORD and wait patiently for Him" (v. 7). For the righteous there is promise; for the unrighteous there is judgment: "The LORD knows the days of the blameless; and their inheritance will be forever. They will not be ashamed in the time of evil, and in the days of famine they will have abundance. But the wicked will perish; and the enemies of the LORD will be like the glory of the pastures, they vanish—like smoke they vanish away" (vv. 18–20).

Jesus said, "Truly I say to you, there is no one who has left house or wife or brothers or parents or children, for the sake of the kingdom of God, who will not receive many times as much at this time and in the age to come, eternal life" (Luke 18:29–30). God irrevocably commits Himself to meet the essential needs of His own.

A Low View of Life

The greatest cause of famine and its attendant diseases in the world is not poor agricultural practices or poor economic and political policies. Nor is the root problem lack of scientific and technological resources or even overpopulation. Those problems only aggravate the basic problem, which is spiritual.

Those parts of the world that have no Christian roots or heritage invariably place a low value on human life. The great poverty and starvation in India, for example, may be laid at the feet of Hinduism, the pagan religion that spawned a host of other religions, including Shintoism and Buddhism. Those religious systems and similar ones spiritually enslave much of the Eastern world, and their influence is gradually spreading to the West.

Because of Hinduism's belief in reincarnation, all animals are considered to be incarnations either of men or deities.

Cows are held especially sacred because supposedly they are incarnated deities, of which Hinduism has 330 million. These cows aggravate the food shortage because they consume 20 percent of India's total food supply. Even rats and mice, which eat 15 percent, are not killed because they might be someone's reincarnated relatives.

Just as paganism is the great plague of India, Africa, and many other parts of the world, Christianity has been the blessing of the West. Europe and the United States, though never fully Christian in any biblical sense, have been immeasurably blessed because of the Christian influence on political, social, and economic philosophy and policy. However, the degraded view of human life, as evidenced in the growing legal and social approval of abortion, infanticide, and euthanasia, and now so widely reflected in the low view of the family, has severely weakened that influence.

A High View of God

Without a proper view of God, there cannot exist a proper view of man. Those who have that right perspective of God also have a right relationship to Him through Jesus Christ, who promised us the provisions of our Heavenly Father. He said:

> Do not be worried about your life, as to what you will eat or what you will drink; nor for your body, as to what you will put on. Is not life more than food, and the body more than clothing? … For the Gentiles eagerly seek all these things; for your heavenly Father knows that you need all these things. But seek first His kingdom and His righteousness, and all these things will be added to you. (Matt. 6:25, 32–33)

As you focus on spiritual matters, God will take care of your physical needs.

Sometimes God has provided for His children through miraculous means, but His primary way of provision is through work (2 Thess. 3:10–12). And He has given us the energy, resources, and opportunity to do so. For those who for whatever legitimate reason are unable to work, He provides care through those who can work. Whether He does so directly or indirectly, God is always the source of our physical well-being. He makes the earth produce what we need, and He gives us the ability to procure it.

One Day at a Time

It is "this day" that we ask God to supply our needs. We are to rely on the Lord one day at a time. To accept the Lord's provision for the present day, without concern for our needs or welfare tomorrow, is a testimony of our contentment in His goodness and faithfulness.

Prayer focuses on God as the One who supplies. It acknowledges that He is the source of all our physical needs, and it teaches us to live one day at a time in the confidence that He will meet those needs.

8

"FORGIVE US OUR DEBTS"

There is an unusual epitaph on a large headstone in a cemetery outside of New York City. The name of the person in the grave is not on the headstone. There is no mention of when the person was born or when the person died. Nor does it indicate anything about the person being a beloved mother, father, husband, wife, brother, sister, son, or daughter. Just one word stretches across the headstone: *Forgiven.* Clearly the most significant fact of this individual's life was the peace he or she knew as a result of God's forgiveness.

Henry Ward Beecher, a popular nineteenth-century American preacher, said:

> Let me saw off a branch from one of the trees that is now budding in my garden, and all summer long there will be an ugly scar where the gash has been made; but by next autumn it will be perfectly

covered over by the growing; and by the following
autumn it will be hidden out of sight; and in four
or five years there will be but a slight scar to show
where it has been; and in ten or twenty years you
would never suspect that there had been an ampu-
tation. Trees know how to overgrow their injuries,
and hide them: and love does not wait so long as
trees do.[1]

The apostle Peter said "love covers a multitude of sins" (1 Peter
4:8), and one of the most important ways it does that is by
forgiveness.

The most essential, blessed, and yet most costly thing God ever
did was to provide man the forgiveness of sin. It is most essential
because it keeps us from hell and gives us joy in this life. It is most
blessed because it introduces us into an eternal fellowship with God.
And it is most costly because the Son of God gave up His life so that
we might live.

John Stott, in his book *Confess Your Sins,* quoted the head of a
large British mental home: "I could dismiss half my patients tomorrow if they could be assured of forgiveness."[2] Deliverance from guilt
by real forgiveness is man's deepest spiritual need. Apart from it, he
can't enter into a relationship with God that produces peace and
hope. He is holy, and His "eyes are too pure to approve evil, and [He]
can not look on wickedness with favor" (Hab. 1:13). "Holy, Holy,
Holy, is the LORD of hosts," said Isaiah (Isa. 6:3). Holy God cannot
possibly entertain a relationship with unholy men unless there is
forgiveness of sin.

That's why our Lord makes it the next topic in His pattern for prayer: "Forgive us our debts, as we also have forgiven our debtors" (Matt. 6:12). Verses 14–15 serve as a footnote: "For if you forgive men for their transgressions, your heavenly Father will also forgive you. But if you do not forgive others, then your Father will not forgive your transgressions."

Sin Is the Problem

Forgiveness of sin is the greatest need of the human heart because sin has a twofold effect: It promises to damn people forever while at the same time robbing them of the fullness of life by burdening the conscience with unrelenting guilt. Ultimately sin separates man from God, thus it is unquestionably the principal enemy and greatest problem of man.

The apostle Paul captured the impact of sin when he quoted several Old Testament passages in his letter to Christians in Rome: "There is none righteous, not even one; there is none who understands, there is none who seeks for God; all have turned aside, together they have become useless; there is none who does good, there is not even one" (Rom. 3:10–12; cf. Ps. 14:1–3; 53:1–4). He then concluded, "All have sinned and fall short of the glory of God" (Rom. 3:23).

The Work of Sin

Sin is the monarch that rules the heart of every man. It is the first lord of the soul, and its virus has contaminated every living being. Sin is the degenerative power in the human stream that makes man susceptible to disease, illness, death, and hell. It is the culprit in every broken marriage, disrupted home, shattered friendship, argument, pain, sorrow, and death. No wonder Scripture compares it to the venom of a snake and the stench of death (Rom. 3:13).

Sin is the moral and spiritual disease for which man has no cure. "Can the Ethiopian change his skin or the leopard his spots? Then you also can do good who are accustomed to do evil" (Jer. 13:23).

- *Sin dominates the mind.* Romans 1:21 indicates that people have reprobate minds given over to evil and lust.

- *Sin dominates the will.* According to Jeremiah 44:15–17, people desire to do evil because their wills are controlled by sin.

- *Sin dominates the emotions and the affections.* Natural people do not want their sins cured because they love darkness rather than light (John 3:19).

- *Sin brings men under the control of Satan.* Ephesians 2:2 teaches that people are guided by "the prince of the power of the air, of the spirit that is now working in the sons of disobedience."

- *Sin brings people under divine wrath.* According to Ephesians 2:3, unsaved people are "children of wrath."

- *Sin subjects men to misery.* Job said, "Man is born for trouble, as sparks fly upward" (Job 5:7). "'There is no peace for the wicked,' says the LORD" (Isa. 48:22).

The Forms of Sin

Five Greek words are typically used by the New Testament writers to refer to some aspect of sin.

Hamartia is the most common and carries the root idea of missing the mark. Sin misses the mark of God's standard of righteousness.

Paraptōma, often rendered "trespass," is the sin of slipping or falling and results more from carelessness than from intentional disobedience.

Parabasis refers to stepping across the line, going beyond the limits prescribed by God. It is often translated "transgression." This sin is more conscious and intentional.

Anomia means "lawlessness" and is an even more intentional and flagrant sin. It describes direct and open rebellion against God and His will.

Opheilēma is the word used in Matthew 6:12. The verb form is used most often to refer to moral or spiritual debts. Sin is a moral or spiritual debt to God that must be paid. In his account of this prayer, Luke uses *hamartia* ("sins"; Luke 11:4), clearly indicating that the reference is to sin, not to financial debt. Matthew probably used *opheilēma* because it corresponded to the most common Aramaic term for sin used by Jews of that day, a term that also represented moral or spiritual debt to God.

Those who trust in Christ have received God's pardon for sin and are saved from eternal hell. Since the Disciples' Prayer is a model for believers to use, the debts referred to there are those incurred by Christians when they sin. Immeasurably more important than our need for daily bread is our need for continual forgiveness of sin. Arthur W. Pink wrote:

> As it is contrary to the holiness of God, sin is a
> defilement, a dishonor, and a reproach to us as it
> is a violation of His law. It is a crime, and as to
> the guilt which we contact thereby, it is a debt.
> As creatures we owe a debt of obedience unto our
> maker and governor, and through failure to render
> the same on account of our rank disobedience, we
> have incurred a debt of punishment; and it is for
> this that we implore a divine pardon.[3]

As a result of our unrelenting sin, we owe a massive debt to God that we could not even begin to pay, much like the debt owed by the unfaithful servant (Matt. 18). Anyone who desires to come to God must do so recognizing the severity of his sin and the magnitude of his debt.

Forgiveness Is the Solution

Since man's severest problem is sin, his greatest need is forgiveness—and that is exactly what God provides. Though we have been forgiven the ultimate penalty of sin through salvation in Christ, we need to experience God's regular forgiveness for the sins we continue to commit. The importance of this distinction will become clearer as we look at the two kinds of forgiveness that we may label judicial and parental.

Judicial Forgiveness

Believers receive God's judicial forgiveness the moment they trust Christ as their Savior from sin. Such forgiveness is comprehensive in the reality of justification, by which God declares us righteous in His Son. As a result, we are no longer under judgment, condemned to die, nor any longer destined for hell. Paul said, "Therefore there is now no condemnation for those who are in Christ Jesus" (Rom. 8:1). The eternal judge has declared us pardoned, justified, and righteous. No one, human or satanic, can condemn us or permanently lay any charge against us (vv. 33–34).

The extent of this forgiveness is mindboggling. God said, "Their sin I will remember no more" (Jer. 31:34). David wrote, "As far as the east is from the west, so far has He removed our transgressions from us" (Ps. 103:12). And Isaiah gave the reason: "The LORD has caused the iniquity of us all to fall on Him [Christ]" (Isa. 53:6; cf. 1 Peter 2:24).

God could not pass by our sin unless He placed the punishment for it on someone else, and that is why Christ died. God has forgiven us (in essence eliminated) our sins based on that onetime sacrifice of Christ on the cross. It was there that He bore our punishment, took our guilt, and paid the penalty for our sin. The moment you place your faith in Christ, your sin is put on Him and His righteousness is put on you, and God judicially declares you justified (Rom. 3:24–26; 2 Cor. 5:21). By that act of judicial forgiveness, all our sins—past, present, and future—are completely forgiven.[4]

Parental Forgiveness

Unfortunately we still fall into sinful behavior because we have not yet been made perfect. In Philippians 3, Paul revealed this distinction when he wrote that through faith in Christ he had received the righteousness of God apart from the law; yet, he added that he had not yet attained a perfect standard of holiness practically (vv. 7–14). So we constantly require forgiveness—the kind that is graciously offered by our Heavenly Father. The apostle John warned us, "If we say that we have no sin, we are deceiving ourselves and the truth is not in us. If we confess our sins, He is faithful and righteous to forgive us our sins and to cleanse us from all unrighteousness" (1 John 1:8–9).

So sin, while it is forgiven judicially, is still a reality in a Christian's life. A decreasing frequency of sin, along with an increasing sensitivity to it, should characterize every Christian's walk. And while our sins today and in the future don't change our standing before God, they do affect the intimacy and joy in our relationship with Him.

For example, if one of your children sinned by disobeying you, that wouldn't change your relationship—you are still his father or mother, ready to forgive instantly. But until he comes to you to confess his disobedience, the prior intimacy will not be restored.

During the Last Supper, Jesus began washing the disciples' feet as a demonstration of the humble, serving spirit that should characterize any of His servants. At first Peter refused, but when Jesus said, "If I do not wash you, you have no part with Me," Peter went to the other extreme and wanted a complete bath. Jesus replied, "He who has bathed needs only to wash his feet, but is completely clean; and you are clean" (John 13:5–10).

Jesus' act of foot washing was more than an example of humility; it was also a picture of the forgiveness God gives in His repeated cleansing of those who are already saved. Dirt on the feet symbolizes the daily surface contamination from sin that we experience as we walk through life. Sin does not, and cannot, make us entirely dirty, because we have been permanently cleansed. The judicial purging that occurs at regeneration needs no repetition, but the practical purification is necessary every day because daily we fall short of God's perfect holiness.

As Judge, God is eager to forgive sinners, and as Father He is even more eager to keep on forgiving His children. Hundreds of years before Christ, Nehemiah wrote, "You are a God of forgiveness, gracious and compassionate, slow to anger, and abounding in lovingkindness" (Neh. 9:17). As vast and pervasive as the sin of man is, the magnitude of God's forgiveness is far greater. Where sin abounds, God's grace abounds even more.

Somewhere in our prayers, after we have asked for His name to be hallowed, His kingdom to come, and His will to be done—and after we have acknowledged that God is the source of our physical and daily sustenance—we need to face the fact that our feet are dirty. As long as we have unconfessed sins in our lives, we will lose fullness of joy and intimacy in our communion with God. Thus the petition "Forgive us our debts" is simply our pleading to God to cleanse us moment by moment when we confess our sins to Him.

Donald Grey Barnhouse, in a conversation with a college professor, told this story that illustrates the magnitude of loving forgiveness:

> A man had lived a life of great sin but had been converted, and eventually had come to marry a fine Christian woman. He had confided to her the nature of his past life in a few words. As he had told her these things, the wife had taken his head

in her hands and had drawn him to her shoulder and had kissed him, saying, "John, I want you to understand something very plainly. I know my Bible well, and therefore I know the subtlety of sin and the devices of sin working in the human heart. I know you are a thoroughly converted man, John, but I know that you still have an old nature, and that you are not yet as fully instructed in the ways of God as you soon will be. The Devil will do all he can to wreck your Christian life, and he will see to it that temptations of every kind will be put in your way. The day might come—please God that it never shall—when you will succumb to temptation and fall into sin. Immediately the Devil will tell you that it is no use trying, that you might as well continue on in the way of sin, and that above all you are not to tell me because it will hurt me. But, John, I want you to know that here in my arms is your home. When I married you, I married your old nature as well as your new nature, and I want you to know there is full pardon and forgiveness in advance for any evil that may ever come into your life."

Dr. Barnhouse said that when he finished the story, the college professor lifted up his eyes reverently and said, "My God! If anything would ever keep a man straight, that [kind of forgiving love] would be it!"[5]

Confession Is Good for the Soul

Asking for forgiveness implies confession. As the apostle John explained, "If we confess our sins, He is faithful and righteous to forgive us our sins and to cleanse us from all unrighteousness" (1 John 1:9). To confess means basically to agree with, and when we confess our sins, we agree with God that they are wicked, evil, and defiling and have no part in those who belong to Him.

It is difficult to confess sins. It's especially hard to get a child to admit he did something wrong. When I was a little boy, another boy and I vandalized a school in an Indiana town where my father was holding a revival meeting. In an attempt to discover who the culprits were, some people went from house to house, seeking information about the perpetrators. When they came to the house where my family was staying, my father and the owner of the house (the other boy's father) answered the door. One of the people asked them if the other boy and I knew anything about the vandalism. I held my father's hand and put on my most angelic face, doing everything I could to show that I was as spiritual as my evangelist father. Both my father and the other father assured the inquirers that we were wonderful boys and would not have been involved in such activity. It took ten years before I built up enough courage to tell my father what had really happened.

Both Satan and our prideful nature fight against any kind of admission to wrongdoing. But confession is the only way to a free and joyful life. Proverbs 28:13 says, "He who conceals his transgressions will not prosper, but he who confesses and forsakes them will find compassion." John Stott says, "One of the surest antidotes to this process of moral hardening is the disciplined practice of uncovering our sins of thought and outlook, as well as word and deed, and the repentant forsaking of them."[6]

If you don't confess your sins, you will become hardened. I've seen Christians—judicially forgiven and eternally secure—who are hardened, impenitent, and insensitive to sin. Consequently, they are also without joy because they don't have a loving, intimate fellowship with God. They have blocked out joy and fellowship with the barricade of their unconfessed sin.

The true Christian does not see God's promise of forgiveness as a license to sin, a way to abuse His love and presume on His grace. Rather, he sees God's gracious forgiveness as the means to spiritual growth and sanctification. He continually thanks God for His great love and willingness to forgive.

Confession of sin is also crucial because it gives God glory when He chastens the disobedient Christian. Such a positive response to His discipline removes any potential complaint of unfairness because the sinner is admitting that he deserves what God gives.

Forgiving Others Is the Ultimate Test

Jesus gives us the prerequisite for forgiving others in the words "as we also have forgiven our debtors" (Matt. 6:12). The principle is simple but sobering: If we have forgiven, we will be forgiven; if we have not forgiven, we will not be forgiven.

Reasons for Forgiving Others

We should forgive one another for several reasons.

A Characteristic of the Saints

As citizens of God's kingdom, we are blessed and receive mercy because we ourselves are merciful (Matt. 5:7). We are to love even our enemies because we have the nature of our Heavenly Father residing in us. Just before giving this model prayer, Jesus instructed His audience, "You have heard that it was said, 'You shall love your neighbor and hate your enemy.' But I say to you, love your enemies and pray for those who persecute you, so that you may be sons of your Father who is in heaven" (Matt. 5:43–45). Blessing those who persecute you is tantamount to forgiveness. By loving your enemies, you manifest that you are a child of God.

Forgiveness is the mark of a truly regenerate heart. When a Christian fails to forgive someone else, he sets himself up as a higher judge than God and even calls into question the reality of his faith.

Christ's Example

The apostle Paul instructed us to "be kind to one another, tender-hearted, forgiving each other, just as God in Christ also has forgiven you" (Eph. 4:32). John told us, "The one who says he abides in Him ought himself to walk in the same manner as He walked" (1 John 2:6). Jesus Himself is our pattern for forgiveness. On behalf of those who drove the nails through His hands, spit in His face, mocked Him, and crushed a crown of thorns onto His head, Jesus said, "Father, forgive them" (Luke 23:34). He is our role model. The severity of any offense toward us cannot match what Christ endured. The writer of Hebrews said, "You have not yet resisted to the point of shedding blood in your striving against sin" (12:4).

Expresses the Highest Virtue of Man

People display the majesty of their creation in the image of God when they forgive. Proverbs 19:11 says, "A man's discretion makes him slow to anger, and it is his glory to overlook a transgression."

Frees the Conscience of Guilt

Unforgiveness not only stands as a barrier to God's forgiveness but also interferes with peace of mind, happiness, satisfaction, and even the proper functioning of the body. According to 2 Corinthians 2:10–11, when we have an unforgiving heart, we give Satan an advantage over us.

Benefits the Body of Believers

Probably few things have so short-circuited the power of the church as unresolved conflicts among its members. The psalmist warned, "If I regard wickedness in my heart, the Lord will not hear" (Ps. 66:18). The Holy Spirit cannot work freely among those who carry grudges and harbor resentment (Matt. 5:23–24).

Delivers from God's Discipline

Where there is an unforgiving spirit, there is sin; and where there is sin, there will be chastening. Hebrews 12:6 says, "Those whom the Lord loves He disciplines, and He scourges every son whom He receives." Unrepentant sin in the church at Corinth caused many believers to be weak, sick, and even to die (1 Cor. 11:30).

Activates God's Forgiveness

The activation of God's forgiveness is probably the most important reason we must forgive others. This reason is so vital that Jesus reinforced it at the close of His pattern for prayer (Matt. 6:14–15). Nothing in the Christian life is more important than forgiveness— our forgiveness of others and God's forgiveness of us. Because God deals with us just as we deal with others, we are to forgive others as freely and graciously as God forgives us.

The Proof of a Forgiving Spirit

As a kind of postscript to the Disciples' Prayer, Matthew 6:14–15 is our Savior's own commentary on the petition of verse 12—the only petition He provides additional insight into. Obviously the truths here are vitally important: "For if you forgive others for their transgressions, your heavenly Father will also forgive you. But if you do not forgive others, then your Father will not forgive your transgressions."

The first part of the principle is positive: "If you forgive others for their transgressions." Believers should forgive as those who have received judicial forgiveness from God. When your heart is filled with such a forgiving spirit, "your heavenly Father will also forgive you." Believers cannot know the parental forgiveness of God, which keeps fellowship with the Lord rich and blessings from Him profuse, apart from forgiving others in heart and word.

The verb translated "forgive" (*aphiimi*) means literally "to hurl away." Paul had that in mind when he wrote, "I found mercy, so that in me as the foremost [of sinners], Jesus Christ might demonstrate His perfect patience" (1 Tim. 1:16; cf. Matt. 7:11). An unforgiving spirit not only is inconsistent for one who has been totally forgiven by God, but it also bears the chastening of God rather than His mercy.

Our Lord illustrated the unmerciful response in the parable of the man forgiven a massive debt (Matt. 18:21–35). "The kingdom of heaven may be compared to a king who wished to settle accounts with his slaves. When he had begun to settle them, one who owed him ten thousand talents was brought to him" (vv. 23–24). One talent was equal to six thousand denarii, and laborers earned one denarius each working day. This slave would have had to work six days a week for one thousand weeks (slightly more than nineteen years) to earn just *one* talent.

You can well imagine that "he did not have the means to repay, [so] his lord commanded him to be sold, along with his wife and children and all that he had, and repayment to be made. So the slave fell to the ground and prostrated himself before him, saying, 'Have patience with me and I will repay you everything'" (vv. 25–26). His debt was massive and would have been impossible for him to repay. Yet "the lord of that slave felt compassion and released him and forgave him the debt" (v. 27). In the symbolism of the parable, the man is forgiven of his unpayable debt, which represents sin, and he finds mercy from the king, which represents salvation. Yet the man abuses this wondrous gift:

> That slave went out and found one of his fellow
> slaves who owed him a hundred denarii; and he
> seized him and began to choke him, saying, "Pay
> back what you owe." So his fellow slave fell to
> the ground and began to plead with him, saying,
> "Have patience with me and I will repay you."
> But he was unwilling and went and threw him in

prison until he should pay back what was owed.
(vv. 28–30)

This debt, while a significant sum (three months' wages), could have been repaid, but it was a trifling amount compared to what the other slave owed. The Lord described what happened next:

> When his fellow slaves saw what had happened, they were deeply grieved and came and reported to their lord all that had happened. Then summoning him, his lord said to him, "You wicked slave, I forgave you all that debt because you pleaded with me. Should you not also have had mercy on your fellow slave, in the same way that I had mercy on you?" And his lord, moved with anger, handed him over to the torturers until he should repay all that was owed him. My heavenly Father will also do the same to you, if each of you does not forgive his brother from your heart. (vv. 31–35)

That is a picture of someone who eagerly receives God's forgiveness but is unwilling to forgive others. I hope you're not holding any grudges and that you have not forgotten the great mercy you have received from God.

Matthew 6:15 captures the essence of this parable and its meaning for believers: "If you do not forgive others, then your Father will not forgive your transgressions." The sin of an unforgiving heart and a bitter spirit (Heb. 12:15) forfeits blessing and invites chastening.

Every believer must seek to manifest the forgiving spirit of Joseph (Gen. 50:19–21) and of Stephen (Acts 7:60) as often as needed. To receive pardon from the perfectly holy God and then refuse to pardon others when we are sinful people is the epitome in abuse of mercy. And "judgment will be merciless to one who has shown no mercy; mercy triumphs over judgment" (James 2:13).

What have we learned? We have an ongoing problem: sin. It interrupts our fellowship and usefulness to our Lord. God's provision for that sin is continual forgiveness. We receive it by confessing our sin. And the prerequisite is that we forgive others. An unforgiving Christian is a proud, selfish person who has forgotten that his sins have been washed away. Learn to confess, and before you confess, learn to forgive. Then we can confidently seek God in the solitude of our hearts and ask Him to forgive us each day.

9

"DELIVER US FROM EVIL"

We live in a fallen world that continually bombards us with the reality of sin and its consequences. We can see it first in the natural world. Volcanoes, earthquakes, fires, floods, pestilences, and accidents are increasing with alarming regularity, threatening the survival of mankind.

The intellectual world in particular assaults our faith. Man is constantly seeking the truth but is unable to find it. His judgments are partial and unfair. His tampering with relative thinking leads to inevitable destruction. Man is propelled by his own self-bias. Logic is ruled by pride, intellects are ruled by lust, and material gain makes liars out of men. Human opinions are on a continual collision course with each other. He has erected fortresses of ideology that are set against truth and God.

Grief and anxiety characterize the emotional world of man. His inability to control destructive attitudes devastates his spirit, and his soul is chafed by his conflicts with others. Envy stings him, hate embitters him, and greed eats away at him like a canker. His affections are misplaced, his love is trampled, and his confidence is betrayed. Rich people step on the poor, and the poor seek to dethrone the rich. Prisons, hospitals, and mental institutions mark the moral and emotional upheaval of man.

But without doubt, the darkest part of man's world is his spiritual life. He is out of harmony with God. The machinery of man's moral nature is visibly out of gear. He is running out of sync with God's divine plan. Evil tendencies dominate man from his tainted, fallen ancestry.

There is seemingly no escape in this world from this for the sincere believer. Wherever we turn, we are confronted by pervasive culture in the fallen world. On top of all that, Satan relentlessly attacks our faith. With such knowledge we must pray, "Do not lead us into temptation, but deliver us from evil" (Matt. 6:13).

Temptation or Trial?

This sixth petition encouragingly speaks of God's protection. At first glance, the interpretation of its meaning seems simple enough: We ask God to keep us out of trouble. But on closer examination, this request is not so simple, and the interpretation is keyed by one word in the Greek text.

Peirasmos ("temptation") is basically a neutral word in Greek, having no necessary connotation either of good or evil, as does our English *temptation,* which refers to inducement to evil. The Greek root deals with a testing or a proving, and from that meaning are derived the related meanings of trial and temptation. Here it seems to parallel the term *evil,* indicating that it has in view enticement to sin.

The Interpretative Problem

God's holiness and goodness will not allow His leading anyone, certainly not one of His children, into a place or experience in which they would purposely be induced to commit sin. James attested to this: "Let no one say when he is tempted, 'I am being tempted by God'; for God cannot be tempted by evil, and He Himself does not tempt anyone" (James 1:13).

Yet James had just said previously, "Consider it all joy, my brethren, when you encounter various trials [*peirasmos*], knowing that the testing of your faith produces endurance" (vv. 2–3). Obviously we are faced with an interpretative problem as to whether *peirasmos* in Matthew 6:13 should be translated "temptation" or "trial." As James told us, God does not tempt. So why ask Him not to do what He would never do anyway? Yet James said we should rejoice when trials come and not seek to avoid them. So why should we pray, "Do not lead us into temptation"?

The Paradoxical Solution

I affirm with Chrysostom, the early church father, that the solution to this issue is that Jesus is not dealing with logic or theology but with a natural appeal of human weakness as it faces danger (*Homily* 19:10). We all desire to avoid the danger and trouble that sin creates. This petition is thus the expression of the redeemed soul that so despises and fears sin that it wants to escape all prospects of falling into it, choosing to avoid rather than having to defeat temptation.

Here is another paradox of Scripture. We know trials are a means to our growing spiritually, morally, and emotionally. Christian character is strengthened by trials. Yet we have no desire to be in a place where the trial might lead to sin. So while we resist trials, we realize that they will strengthen us because they exercise our spiritual muscles.

Even Jesus, when He prayed in the garden of Gethsemane, first asked, "My Father, if it is possible, let this cup pass from Me," before He said, "yet not as I will, but as You will" (Matt. 26:39). Jesus was horrified at the prospect of taking sin upon Himself, yet He was willing to endure it to fulfill the will of His Father, which was to bring about the redemption of sinners who embrace the Son.

Our proper reaction to times of temptation is similar to Christ's, but for us it is primarily a matter of self-distrust. When we honestly look at the power of sin and at our own weakness and sinful propensities, we shudder at the danger of temptation or even trial. That was what James was getting at when he said, "Each one is tempted when he is carried away and enticed by his own lust. Then when lust has conceived, it gives birth to sin; and when sin is accomplished, it brings forth death" (James 1:14–15).

This petition is thus another plea for God to provide what we in ourselves do not have. It is an appeal to God to place a watch over our eyes, our ears, our mouths, our feet, and our hands—that in whatever we see, hear, or say, and in any place we go and in anything we do, He will protect us from sin. And when we are tempted, we need to remember that "every good thing given and every perfect gift is from above, coming down from the Father of lights, with whom there is no variation or shifting shadow" (James 1:17).

Pass or Fail?

When we speak of a trial or test, we will either pass or fail. Thus every trial God allows can turn into a temptation. Long after Joseph's brothers sold him into slavery in Egypt, he told them, "You meant evil against me, but God meant it for good" (Gen. 50:20). Every struggle and trial we experience is allowed by God to test us, to exercise our spiritual muscles, and to help us mature (cf. 1 Peter 5:10). But if you don't commit the situation to God and stand in His strength, Satan will turn it into a temptation. He will entice your lusts and may draw you into sin.

Dealing with Trials

We are not certain that, like Joseph, we will be completely submissive to and dependent on God in our trials. The implication of this part of the prayer seems to be: "Lord, don't ever lead us into a trial that will present such a temptation that we will not be able to resist it. Rather, deliver us from any trial that would bring evil on us as a natural consequence. Don't put us into something we can't handle." This is laying claim to the promise, "God is faithful, who will not allow you to be tempted beyond what you are able, but with the temptation will provide the way of escape also, so that you will be able to endure it" (1 Cor. 10:13).

While God won't tempt us to sin, He will bring things into our lives that become tests for us. When you pass a certain magazine, book, movie theater, or program on your television, that can be a test to reveal your spiritual strength. If you fail, it will turn into a temptation that incites your lust and draws you into sin.

If you're terminated from your job, that may be a test. How are you going to handle it? If you take it joyously and commit your situation to the Lord, you will pass the test. But Satan will tempt you to complain and perhaps to do all you can to ruin your boss's reputation.

Matthew 4:1 says Jesus was "led up by the Spirit into the wilderness to be tempted by the devil." To God it was a test to prove Christ's virtue; for Satan it was a temptation to destroy His virtue. Job said, "When He has tried me, I shall come forth as gold" (Job 23:10). He approached his trial the right way. Peter said, "In this you greatly rejoice, even though now for a little while, if necessary, you have been distressed by various trials, so that the proof of your faith, being more precious than gold which is perishable, even though tested by fire, may be found to result in praise and glory and honor at the revelation of Jesus Christ" (1 Peter 1:6–7).

The Lord orders our lives so that we will never be tempted without the strength to resist (1 Cor. 10:13). He uses our trials to help us trust Him more and strengthen others who go through the same trial later. He also uses them to drive us to His Word and to prayer.

The petition in Matthew 6:13 is a safeguard against presumption and a false sense of security and self-sufficiency. We know that we will never have arrived spiritually and that we will never be free of the danger of sin until we are with the Lord. As our dear Lord prayed for us in His great intercessory prayer, we want, at all costs, to be kept from the evil one (John 17:15).

Dealing with Temptation

When we sincerely pray "Do not lead us into temptation, but deliver us from evil," we also declare our submission to God's Word, which is our protection from sin. James 4:7 gives us a simple command: "Submit therefore to God. Resist the devil and he will flee from you." Submitting to God is submitting to His Word: "Your word I have treasured in my heart, that I may not sin against You" (Ps. 119:11). So the believer prays to be kept from overwhelming solicitation into sin, and if he falls into it, he prays to be rescued from it.

In a cursed world where we are continually battered by wickedness all around us, we confess our inadequacy to deal with such evil. We confess the weakness of our flesh and the absolute impotency of human resources to combat sin and rescue us from its clutches. Above all we confess our need for the protection and deliverance of our loving Heavenly Father.

Will God honor the petition in Matthew 6:13? According to 1 Corinthians 10:13, He will. God will never allow us to experience trials that are more than we can handle. That is seen in Matthew 6:13 in the phrase "deliver us from evil." God will never let us be tempted above what we are able to endure. That's His promise, and if we meet the condition of that promise, we can claim it. What is the condition? Submit yourself to the Lord and resist the devil.

What have we learned from the Lord's Prayer? All that we need is available to us. First we are to give God His rightful place. Then we can bring our needs to Him, and He will meet them through His limitless, eternal supply. An unknown author summarized well the impact of this pattern for prayer:

> I cannot say "our" if I live only for myself in a spiritual, watertight compartment.
>
> I cannot say "Father" if I do not endeavor each day to act like His child. I cannot say "who art in heaven" if I am laying up no treasure there. I cannot

say "hallowed be Thy name" if I am not striving for holiness.

I cannot say "Thy kingdom come" if I am not doing all in my power to hasten that wonderful day.

I cannot say "Thy will be done" if I am disobedient to His Word. I cannot say "on earth as it is in heaven" if I will not serve Him here and now. I cannot say "give us ... our daily bread" if I am dishonest or an "under-the-counter" shopper. I cannot say "forgive us our debts" if I harbor a grudge against anyone.

I cannot say "lead us not into temptation" if I deliberately place myself in its path.

I cannot say "deliver us from evil" if I do not put on the whole armor of God.

I cannot say "Thine is the kingdom" if I do not give to the King the loyalty due Him as a faithful subject.

I cannot attribute to Him "the power" if I fear what men may do.

I cannot ascribe to Him "the glory" if I am seeking honor only for myself.

I cannot say "forever" if the horizon of my life is bounded completely by the things of time.

As you commit to following this pattern for all your prayers, your entire Christian walk will be revolutionized, not just your prayer life. No longer will you lack for something to say in prayer. Being alone with God will never be the same.

Part Three

PRAYER IN ACTION

10

PRAYING FOR THE RIGHT THINGS

When you pray, what do you typically pray for? If we were to take a survey of the evangelical church today on the topics most often prayed for, we would discover that most prayers are often misdirected, shortsighted, and selfish. We typically pray for health, happiness, and success. We pray for personal comfort. We pray for solutions to remedy all the physical problems of life, such as: healing, a place to live, a job, a car, a husband, a wife, children, a promotion, more money, and so on. As important as those things are, in some respects (especially to the people in need), they are low on the priority list in God's kingdom. Jesus said we are not to be anxious about what we eat, drink, or wear when we know God supplies them all (Matt. 6:25–33). Our priority must be with the advancement of God's kingdom.

We live in a world that knows little about what's truly valuable. People all around us are pursuing things that have no lasting value.

That pursuit is ably treated by Anton Chekhov in his classic short story *The Bet*. This story gives us great insight into the value system of most people.

The plot involves a wager between two educated men regarding solitary confinement. A wealthy, middle-aged banker believed the death penalty was a more humane penalty than solitary confinement because "an executioner kills at once, solitary confinement kills gradually." One of his guests at a party, a young lawyer of twenty-five, disagreed, saying, "To live under any conditions is better than not to live at all."

Angered, the banker impulsively responded with a bet of two million rubles that the younger man could not last five years in solitary confinement. The lawyer was so convinced of his endurance that he announced he would stay fifteen years alone instead of only five.

The arrangements were made, and the young man moved into a separate building on the grounds of the banker's large estate. He was allowed no visitors or newspapers. He could write letters but receive none. There were guards watching to make sure he never violated the agreement, but they were placed so that he could never see another human being from his windows. He received his food in silence through a small opening where he could not see those who served him. Everything else he wanted—books, certain foods, musical instruments, etc.—was granted by special written request.

During the first year his guards could hear him playing the piano at almost any hour, and he asked for many books, mostly novels and other light reading. The next year the music ceased, and he requested the works of various classical authors. In the sixth year of his isolation, he began to study languages and soon had mastered six. After the tenth year of his confinement, the prisoner sat motionless at the table and read the New Testament. After more than a year's saturation of the Bible, he began to study the history of religion and works on theology.

The second half of the story focuses on the night before the noon deadline when the lawyer would win the bet. The banker was now at the end of his career. His risky speculations and impetuosity had gradually undermined his business. The once self-confident millionaire was now a second-rate banker, and it would destroy him to pay off the wager. Angry at his foolishness and jealous of the soon-to-be-wealthy lawyer who was now only forty, the old banker determined to kill his opponent and frame the guard with the murder. Slipping into the man's room, he found him asleep at the table and noticed a letter the lawyer had written to him. He picked it up and read the following:

> Tomorrow at twelve o'clock I shall be free … but before leaving this room … I find it necessary to say a few words to you. With a clear conscience, and before God, who sees me, I declare to you that I despise freedom and life and health and all that your books call the joys of this world.… I know I am wiser than you all.… And I despise all your books, I despise all earthly blessings and wisdom. All is worthless and false, hollow and deceiving like the mirage. You may be proud, wise and beautiful, but death will wipe you away from the face of the earth, as it does the mice that live beneath your

floor; and your heirs, your history, your immortal
geniuses will freeze or burn with the destruction of
the earth. You have gone mad and are not following
the right path. You take falsehood for truth, and
deformity for beauty. To prove to you how I despise
all that you value I renounce the two million on
which I looked, at one time, as the opening of
paradise for me, and which I now scorn. To deprive
myself of the right to receive them, I will leave my
prison five hours before the appointed time, and by
so doing break the terms of our compact.

The banker read the lines, replaced the paper on the table, kissed
the strange, sleeping man, and with tears in his eyes quietly left the
house. Chekhov wrote, "Never before, not even after sustaining serious
losses on change, had he despised himself as he did at that moment."
His tears kept him awake the rest of the night. And at seven the next
morning, he was informed by the watchmen that they had seen the
man crawl through a window, go to the gate, and then disappear.

Some people have to learn the hard way what is of value, and
there are some who never learn.

We have just spent several chapters learning what is of value in
our prayers. Jesus' pattern for prayer in Matthew 6:9–15 gave us the
framework on which we can build our own practice of prayer. In these
two remaining chapters, we will look at the specific spiritual issues that
ought to be the focus of our prayers. These issues will expand and flesh
out the pattern Jesus gave. To understand such vital matters, we will
need to explore what the apostle Paul taught concerning them.

Paul knew what was important in the Christian life. His prayers for the saints are striking for their exclusive treatment of spiritual concerns. One of his prayers in particular stands out for its simplicity and its depth: "We pray for you always, that our God will count you worthy of your calling, and fulfill every desire for goodness and the work of faith with power" (2 Thess. 1:11). Paul often focused his prayers on the issues that would abound to the spiritual benefit of the saints. Here he had three wishes for the Thessalonians: worthiness, fulfillment, and powerful service.

The Resource

Before we look at those three requests and their implications, we need to consider briefly the resource of all spiritual blessing. Most of what Paul desired for the saints he knew he could obtain only by prayer. He did not turn to human ingenuity or some program; he turned to God. Paul was a faithful shepherd who taught God's people whenever and wherever he could the importance of obeying His commands. But that in itself was not enough—he had to turn to God, who alone could prompt that obedience in the people. Paul knew that God desires to sanctify His people, and that was his desire as well. Therefore, he prayed for the things God wanted to accomplish in His people.

If you want to pray for one another, don't pray for the physical necessities only—make it your priority to pray for the important spiritual issues of life because they are of the greatest concern to God. His ultimate purpose is to conform you to the image of Jesus Christ. The little tests and trials in life are important only insofar as they reveal your greater spiritual need. God is most concerned about your response and attitude toward events that occur in your life.

For Paul, and for any mature Christian, prayer is a permanent state of mind by which the promises and purposes of God, the spiritual well-being of His people, the advance of His gospel, and the growth of His church are passionately desired. What concerns the Lord must concern you if you truly desire to glorify Him in your life.

The Requests

Paul's prayer for the Thessalonians contains three vital and dynamic spiritual issues that are critical for all believers: "That our God will count you worthy of your calling, and fulfill every desire for goodness and the work of faith with power" (2 Thess. 1:11). Worthiness refers to spiritual character. It should be our desire that the Lord would make us the kind of people we ought to be. Fulfillment speaks of God bringing about in our lives every holy longing. And power is necessary for our service to be truly effective. When you pray for your loved ones or for fellow brothers and sisters in Christ, pray for their worthiness, fulfillment, and power in service. When those issues are the priorities of our prayers and our patterns of obedience, God will be honored.

Worthiness

Paul's first request is that God "will count you worthy of your calling." This is a broad request that encompasses our Christian character. If we claim to belong to Christ, we need to live in such a way that honors Him.

The phrase *your calling* is a rich New Testament concept that always, in the epistles, refers to the effectual saving call that results in regeneration. This is not a call to repent or believe. It is the calling Paul described in Romans: "Whom He predestined, He also called; and these whom He called, He also justified; and these whom He justified; He also glorified" (Rom. 8:30). Here, *calling* takes its place in the flow of salvation—the "calling" that activates in time the election in eternity past. And it is an irrevocable call (Rom. 11:29). In his first epistle to the Thessalonians, Paul discussed the importance of this calling: "So that you would walk in a manner worthy of the God who calls you into His own kingdom and glory" (1 Thess. 2:12).

Paul's point is clear. Believers have been called to salvation—to bear the name Christian and become identified as God's people. So he prayed for us to be deserving of bearing Christ's name.

Worthiness in Position

All are worthy of death and unworthy of salvation. That was true of us before God saved us. Thus we can conclude that God saves the unworthy and makes them worthy. That is our position in Christ. Just as you were declared righteous in the righteousness of Christ, so you were called worthy because of His righteousness. You didn't earn your righteousness; neither did you earn your worthiness—it is all yours through God's grace gift only. So in your positional standing before God you are worthy.

Worthiness in Practice

It is in the practical sense that Paul asked God to count us worthy of our calling. God wants you to bear His name honorably, and He will use your suffering to accomplish that goal: "This is a plain indication of God's righteous judgment so that you may be considered worthy of the kingdom of God, for which indeed you are suffering" (2 Thess. 1:5). The suffering He ushers into your life peels away the flesh and drives you to Himself. And that ultimately brings spiritual maturity.

To be counted worthy of our calling should be the prayer of every believer. We all should desire that no believer bring reproach on Christ or dishonor His name. Paul had to specifically address a group of people in the church at Thessalonica who were doing that very thing: "We command you, brethren, in the name of our Lord Jesus Christ, that you keep away from every brother who leads an unruly life and not according to the tradition which you received from us" (2 Thess. 3:6). Some believers evidently were not obedient to God's Word and the teaching of the apostles and were leading an unruly life instead. In fact, some were "leading an undisciplined life, doing no work at all, but acting like busybodies" (v. 11). They may have been worthy in their positional standing before Christ, but they certainly weren't living in a way that practically honored Him.

You and I have an immeasurable privilege and responsibility to bear the name of Christ in a worthy manner. This was a consistent theme throughout Paul's epistles. To the Ephesians he wrote, "Therefore I, the prisoner of the Lord, implore you to walk in a manner worthy of the calling with which you have been called, with all humility and gentleness, with patience, showing tolerance to one another in love, being diligent to preserve the unity of the Spirit in the bond of peace" (Eph. 4:1–3).

To the Philippians he said, "Only conduct yourselves in a manner worthy of the gospel of Christ … standing firm in one spirit, with one mind striving together for the faith of the gospel; in no way alarmed by your opponents" (Phil. 1:27–28).

And to the Colossians he wrote, "That you will walk in a manner worthy of the Lord, to please Him in all respects, bearing fruit in every good work and increasing in the knowledge of God; strengthened with all power, according to His glorious might" (Col. 1:10–11). Each of those passages gives us some insight into the particulars of a worthy walk—a life we should strive to follow and characteristics we should ask God to make prevalent in all our lives.

The following is a New Testament list of all that is encompassed in a worthy walk:

- Humility (Eph. 4:2–3)

- Purity (Rom. 13:13)

- Contentment (1 Cor. 7:17)

- Faith (2 Cor. 5:7)

- Righteousness (Eph. 2:10)

- Unity (Phil. 1:27)

- Gentleness (Eph. 4:2)

- Patience (Col. 1:11)

- Love (Eph. 5:2)

- Joy (Col. 1:11)

- Thankfulness (Col. 1:3)

- Light (Eph. 5:8–9)

- Knowledge (Col. 1:10)

- Wisdom (Eph. 5:15–16)

- Truth (3 John vv. 3–4)

- Fruitfulness (Col. 1:10)

If you truly belong to Christ, you ought to walk as He walked (1 John 2:6).

Fulfillment

Paul's second request is for God to "fulfill every desire for goodness." The Greek word translated "fulfill" (*pleroō*) means "to accomplish." So Paul is asking God to accomplish in our lives every desire that is good by His definition.

The Psalms often reflect this desire. David prayed, "You have given him his heart's desire, and You have not withheld the request of his lips. For You meet him with the blessings of good things" (Ps. 21:2–3). He also said, "Delight yourself in the LORD; and He will give you the desires of your heart" (37:4). Will God give you everything your heart desires? He will as long as your delight is in Him and your desires are His desires. This bold statement verifies that truth: "The LORD will accomplish what concerns me" (138:8). How could David be so confident? Because his agenda was the same as God's agenda.

I'm sure many people assume God is reluctant to make anyone happy—that He receives some measure of satisfaction by leaving people in permanent misery to remind them He's stringent and demanding. But that's not true at all. God wants to give you the desire of your heart as long as your desire is consistent with His. Psalm 145:16 indicates that God satisfies the desire of every living thing. God is generous and gracious. He longs to give His children what they desire, but only when it is a righteous desire.

Power

Paul's third request is for God to "fulfill ... the work of faith with power." The Thessalonian believers already were involved in the work of faith (2 Thess. 1:3–5). Their faith was real because it produced fruit. But Paul wanted to see them enlarge their faith, so he prayed for their faith to be more powerful.

Paul prayed that way for the Ephesians: "That He would grant you, according to the riches of His glory, to be strengthened with power through His Spirit in the inner man" (Eph. 3:16). The power of God is released in you when you allow God's Word to dominate your life (Col. 3:16).

What you pray for your spouse, for your children, for your friends, for the people you love should not be limited to temporal things. Instead ask God to make their work of faith powerful, fulfill their longings for goodness, and cause their lives to be worthy to bear the name of Christ.

The Reason

Our reason to pray for such spiritual benefits is a fairly obvious one—one that we have affirmed again and again in this book: "so that the name of our Lord Jesus will be glorified in you, and you in Him, according to the grace of our God and the Lord Jesus Christ" (2 Thess. 1:12). That is the ultimate reason we do anything in the Christian life. If that isn't our ultimate goal, we're focusing too much on ourselves (cf. John 14:13–14).

We pray for each other to be worthy of our calling because Christ's reputation is at stake. That was Daniel's perspective when he prayed, "O Lord, hear! O Lord, forgive! O Lord, listen and take action! For Your own sake, O my God, do not delay, because Your city and Your people are called by Your name" (Dan. 9:19).

One of the primary excuses people give for rejecting Christianity is hypocrisy manifest in the Christians they have met. Thus Paul prayed that we will be the opposite of hypocrites—that we will bring honor to the name of Christ and lead unbelievers to Him as a result. That's why Jesus said, "Let your light shine before men in such a way that they may see your good works, and glorify your Father who is in heaven" (Matt. 5:16). Paul's desire here is expressed no better than in his second epistle to the Corinthians: "As for Titus, he is my partner and fellow worker among you; as for our brethren, they are messengers of the churches, a glory to Christ" (2 Cor. 8:23).

I hope you'll begin to give priority to the important spiritual matters. But to do so is not easy since our tendency is to focus on the temporal. However, placing spiritual concerns first is a sacrifice well worth making. To help you, consider the following example of sacrifice:

> The Pony Express was a private express company
> that carried mail by an organized relay of horseback
> riders. The eastern end was St. Joseph, Missouri,

and the western terminal was in Sacramento, California. The cost of sending a letter by Pony Express was $2.50 an ounce. If the weather and horses held out and the Indians held off, that letter would complete the entire two-thousand-mile journey in a speedy ten days, as did the report of Lincoln's inaugural address.

It may surprise you that the Pony Express was only in operation from April 3, 1860 to November 18, 1861—just seventeen months. When the telegraph line was completed between the two cities, the service was no longer needed.

Being a rider for the Pony Express was a tough job. You were expected to ride seventy-five to one hundred miles a day, changing horses every fifteen to twenty-five miles. Other than the mail, the only baggage you carried contained a few provisions, including a kit of flour, cornmeal, and bacon. In case of danger, you also had a medical pack of turpentine, borax, and cream of tartar. In order to travel light and to increase speed of mobility during Indian attacks, the men always rode in shirtsleeves, even during the fierce winter weather.

How would you recruit volunteers for this hazardous job? An 1860 San Francisco newspaper printed this ad for the Pony Express: "WANTED: Young, skinny, wiry fellows not over 18. Must be expert riders willing to risk daily. Orphans preferred."[1]

11

PRAYING FOR THE LOST

Charles Spurgeon related well the priority all Christians must give to praying for the lost:

> *The soul-winner must be a master of the art of prayer.* You cannot bring souls to God if you go not to God yourself. You must get your battle-ax, and your weapons of war, from the armoury of sacred communication with Christ. If you are much alone with Jesus, you will catch His Spirit; you will be fired with the flame that burned in His breast, and consumed His life. You will weep with the tears that fell upon Jerusalem when He saw it perishing; and if you cannot speak so eloquently as He did, yet shall there be about what you say somewhat of the same power which in Him thrilled the hearts and awoke

the consciences of men. My dear hearers, especially you members of the church, I am always so anxious lest any of you should begin to lie upon your oars, and take things easy in the matters of God's kingdom. There are some of you—I bless you, and I bless God at the remembrance of you—who are in season, and out of season, in earnest for winning souls, and you are the truly wise; but I fear there are others whose hands are slack, who are satisfied to let me preach, but do not themselves preach; who take these seats, and occupy these pews, and hope the cause goes well, but that is all they do.[1]

What Christian does not pray for the salvation of friends and loved ones who do not know the Lord? Yet we must have a broader outlook than that. Scripture supports the perspective that we should all pray for the lost in general.

The Bible gives several examples of prayer for those outside salvation. In Numbers 14:19, Moses prayed, "Pardon, I pray, the iniquity of this people according to the greatness of Your lovingkindness, just as You also hast forgiven this people, from Egypt even until now." He cried out to God for the forgiveness of the sinning Israelites.

Samuel the prophet also prayed for Israel's salvation. In 1 Samuel 7:3–5 we read:

Then Samuel spoke to all the house of Israel, saying, "If you return to the LORD with all your heart, remove the foreign gods and the Ashtaroth from

among you and direct your hearts to the LORD and
serve Him alone; and He will deliver you from
the hand of the Philistines." So the sons of Israel
removed the Baals and the Ashtaroth and served
the LORD alone. Then Samuel said, "Gather all
Israel to Mizpah, and I will pray to the LORD for
you."

Later in 1 Samuel, after rebuking them for their sin in demanding a king, he said, "Moreover, as for me, far be it from me that I
should sin against the LORD by ceasing to pray for you; but I will
instruct you in the good and right way" (12:23).

The New Testament relates the testimony of Stephen. While
being stoned to death, he prayed what amounted to a prayer for
his executioners' salvation: "They went on stoning Stephen as he
called upon the Lord and said, 'Lord Jesus, receive my spirit!'
Then falling on his knees, he cried out with a loud voice, 'Lord,
do not hold this sin against them!' Having said this, he fell asleep"
(Acts 7:59–60).

Paul had a deep desire for the salvation of his fellow Israelites.
He expressed that desire in Romans 9:1–4: "I am telling the truth in
Christ, I am not lying, my conscience testifies with me in the Holy
Spirit, that I have great sorrow and unceasing grief in my heart. For
I could wish that I myself were accursed, separated from Christ for
the sake of my brethren, my kinsmen according to the flesh, who are
Israelites." That deep concern could not help but find expression in
his prayer life: "Brethren, my heart's desire and my prayer to God for
them is for their salvation" (Rom. 10:1).

The Bible, then, clearly expresses the appropriateness and propriety of praying for the lost. In addition to the examples noted above, evangelistic praying is the express teaching of 1 Timothy 2:1–8. These verses are polemical in nature; they confront a problem in the Ephesian church. Since Paul here commanded prayer for the lost, we may conclude that such praying had slipped from the priority it should have been at Ephesus.

Since the scope of the gospel call is universal, Paul showed the need to pray for all men. The goal of the church, like Israel before it, is to reach the world with the saving truth of God. Israel failed to be the faithful nation by which God could reach the world, and the responsibility has been passed to the church. Paul wrote out of concern that the exclusivity that caused Israel to fail in her mission should not cripple the church. However, history shows that the church has, in fact, become content with itself and often neglectful of sinners.

The central function of the church on earth is to reach the lost. Paul knew that the Ephesians would never do that as long as they maintained their selfish exclusivism. To carry out their mission in the world, they must be made to understand the breadth of the gospel call. And the first feature in understanding that is to come to grips with evangelistic praying.

The Nature of Evangelistic Prayer

Paul wrote, "First of all, then, I urge that entreaties and prayers, petitions and thanksgivings, be made" (1 Tim. 2:1). While the first three terms Paul uses are virtually synonymous, there are among them some subtle shades of meaning that enrich our concept of prayer. *Entreaties* refers to prayer that arises from a sense of need. Knowing what is lacking, we plead with God to supply it. As we look out on the masses of lost humanity, the enormity of the need should drive us to our knees in evangelistic prayer.

The seventeenth-century English Puritan Richard Baxter wrote:

> Oh, if you have the hearts of Christians or of men in you, let them yearn towards your poor ignorant, ungodly neighbours. Alas, there is but a step betwixt them and death and hell; many hundred diseases are waiting ready to seize on them, and if they die unregenerate, they are lost forever. Have you hearts of rock, that cannot pity men in such a case as this? If you believe not the Word of God, and the danger of sinners, why are you Christians yourselves? If you do believe it, why do you not bestir yourself to the helping of others? Do you not care who is damned, so you be saved? If so, you have sufficient cause to pity yourselves, for it is a frame of spirit utterly inconsistent with grace…. Dost thou live close by them, or meet them in the streets, or labour with them, or travel with them, or sit and talk with them, and say nothing to them of their souls, or the life to come? If their houses were on fire, thou wouldst run and help them; and wilt thou not help them when their souls are almost at the fire of hell?[2]

Prayers refers simply to prayer in general. Unlike *entreaties,* in Scripture the term is used only in reference to God. It thus carries with it a unique element of worship and reverence. Prayer for the lost is ultimately directed at God as an act of worship, because the salvation of sinners causes them to give glory to Him.

The Greek word translated *petitions* comes from a root word meaning "to fall in with someone." The verb form is used to speak of both Christ's and the Spirit's intercession for us (Heb. 7:25; Rom. 8:26). The Members of the Trinity identify with our needs and become involved in our struggles, revealing empathy, sympathy, and compassion. Praying for the lost should never be cold, detached, or impersonal, like a public defender assigned to represent a defendant. Understanding the depths of their misery and pain, and their coming doom, we must cry to God for the salvation of sinners.

Thanksgivings is the fourth element in evangelistic prayers. We pray with a spirit of gratitude to God that the gospel offer has been extended, that we have the privilege of reaching the lost with that gospel, and that some respond with faith and repentance.

These four nuances enrich our prayers as we pray effectively for the lost. If they are missing, we need to examine our hearts. Do we fully realize the desperate condition the lost are in? Do we really want to see God glorified by the salvation of souls? Do we sympathize with the compelling reality of their lost souls, both for time and eternity? Are we thankful the gospel message is extended to all and for our privilege of sharing it? If those components are lacking in our hearts, we will be indifferent. Often we are indifferent simply because we are not obedient to those urgings.

The Scope of Evangelistic Prayer

We are to offer those prayers "on behalf of all men, for kings and all who are in authority" (1 Tim. 2:1–2). As we discovered in the previous chapter, our prayers are all too often narrowly confined to personal needs and wants and rarely extend beyond those of our immediate circle of friends and family. In sharp contrast, however, Paul called for evangelistic prayer "on behalf of all men." There is no place for selfishness or exclusivity. We are not to try to limit either the gospel call or our evangelistic prayers to the elect. After all, we have no means of knowing who the elect are until they respond to the gospel call. Moreover, we are told that God desires all to be saved (2:4). He takes no pleasure in the death of the wicked, but rather delights when sinners turn from their evil ways and live (Ezek. 33:11). So prayer for the salvation of the lost is perfectly consistent with the heart of God. He has commanded all men to repent (Acts 17:30). We must pray that they will do so, and that they will embrace the salvation offered to all (Titus 2:11).

Out of the universal group of "all men," Paul specifically singled out some who might otherwise be neglected in evangelistic prayer: "kings and all who are in authority." Because ancient (and modern) rulers are so often tyrannical, and even disrespectful of the Lord and His people, they are targets of bitterness and animosity. They are also remote, not part of the everyday lives of believers. Hence there is a tendency to be indifferent toward them.

To neglect them is a serious sin because of the authority and responsibility leaders have. Paul's injunction here called for the Ephesian assembly to pray for the emperor, who at that time was the cruel and vicious blasphemer Nero. Although he was a vile, debauched persecutor of the faith, they were still to pray for his redemption. For the sake of their eternal souls, we should pray that all "kings and all who are in authority" would repent of their sins and believe the gospel.

Paul did not command us to pray for the removal from office of evil rulers or those with whom we disagree politically. We are to be loyal and submissive to our government (Rom. 13:1–5; 1 Peter 2:17). If the church today took the effort it spends on political maneuvering and lobbying and poured that energy into intercessory prayer, we might see a profound impact on our nation. We all too often forget that "the weapons of our warfare are not of the flesh, but divinely powerful for the destruction of fortresses" (2 Cor. 10:4). The key to changing a nation is the salvation of sinners, and that calls for faithful prayer.

The Benefit of Evangelistic Prayer

The benefit to praying for the lost is actually quite profound: "so that we may lead a tranquil and quiet life in all godliness and dignity" (1 Tim. 2:2). Prayer for those in authority will create societal conditions favorable for the church's evangelistic efforts. First of all, when believers are committed to praying for all their leaders, it removes any thought of rebellion or resistance against them. Instead the people of Christ are turned into peacemakers, not reactionaries. As Paul wrote to Titus:

> Remind them to be subject to rulers, to authorities,
>   to be obedient, to be ready for every good deed,

to malign no one, to be peaceable, gentle, showing every consideration for all men. For we also
once were foolish ourselves, disobedient, deceived,
enslaved to various lusts and pleasures, spending
our life in malice and envy, hateful, hating one
another. (Titus 3:1–3)

Here Paul again called the believers to tranquility and submis-
siveness to the pagan or apostate governments over them. We can do
so because we understand that they are sinners like we used to be,
incapable of righteousness.

When believers begin to pray unceasingly for the lost, especially
their troublesome leaders, unbelievers begin to see Christians as
virtuous, peace-loving, compassionate, and transcendent, seeking
after their welfare. Once unsaved people realize we pose no threat
to society, it is easier for us to be treated as welcome friends. And
as more come to saving faith through the prayers of Christians, the
favorable conditions for the church could increase.

The Absence of Disturbance

The church that is obedient to this mandate will "lead a tranquil
and quiet life." The Greek words translated "tranquil" and "quiet"
are rare adjectives. The former, appearing only here in the New
Testament, refers to the absence of outside disturbances. The latter,
appearing only here and in 1 Peter 3:4, refers to the absence of internal disturbances. When the church manifests its love and goodness
toward all and pours itself into compassionate, concerned prayer for
the lost, it will lessen the hostility that may exist toward it. As a

result, the saints may enjoy freedom from both internal and external disturbances.

The church, while remaining uncompromising in its commitment to the truth, is not to be the agitator and disrupter of the national life. That is the clear teaching of Scripture. If we are persecuted, it must be for Christ's sake, for the sake of righteous living (cf. 1 Peter 2:13–23).

In 1 Thessalonians 4:11, Paul commanded the Thessalonian believers "to make it your ambition to lead a quiet life and attend to your own business and work with your hands." Christians are to be known for their quiet demeanor, not for making disturbances. Unbelievers should see us as quiet, loyal, diligent, virtuous people. Although we may hate the evil world system that is the enemy of God, we are not to see those in it as our personal enemies. They are captives of the real enemy, the devil (cf. 2 Tim. 2:24–26). They are not our enemies; they are our mission field.

The Presence of Holiness

To promote a "tranquil and quiet life," believers must pursue "godliness and dignity." *Godliness* translates *"eusebeia,"* a common word in the Pastoral Epistles. It carries the idea of reverence toward God. Believers should live for the majesty, holiness, love, and glory of God.

Semnotēs, translated "dignity," could be translated "moral earnestness." *Godliness* can refer to a proper attitude, *dignity* to proper behavior. Thus believers are to be marked by a commitment to morality; holy motives must result in holy behavior. Both contribute to the tranquility and quietness of our lives.

That is not to say, however, that the Christian life will be free of problems. "Indeed," Paul wrote in 2 Timothy 3:12, "all who desire to live godly in Christ Jesus will be persecuted." The Christian life is a war against Satan and the forces of evil. Paul himself was beaten and imprisoned for his faith. His point in this passage, however, is that if we incur animosity and suffer persecution, it is to be for nothing other than our godly attitude and behavior. We must not provoke negative responses by being a disruptive force in society.

The Reasons for Evangelistic Prayer

Why should we pray for the lost? Paul gave the answer in one of the most powerful and dramatic passages in all Scripture on the saving purpose of God:

> This is good and acceptable in the sight of God our Savior, who desires all men to be saved and to come to the knowledge of the truth. For there is one God, and one mediator also between God and men, the man Christ Jesus, who gave Himself as a ransom for all, the testimony given at the proper time. For this I was appointed a preacher and an apostle (I am telling the truth, I am not lying) as a teacher of the Gentiles in faith and truth. (1 Tim. 2:3–7)

Morally Right

God defines prayer for the lost as the noble and spiritually proper thing to do, and our consciences agree. The lost suffer the agony of sin, shame, and meaninglessness in this life and the unrelenting agony of eternal hell in the life to come. Knowing that, our most excellent task is to pray for their salvation.

Some might argue the contrary, pointing out that Jesus said in John 17:9, "I do not ask on behalf of the world." But there, Christ was praying as the great High Priest for God's elect. Because He is the sovereign, omniscient Deity, His prayer was specific in a way ours cannot be. He was praying exclusively for the salvation of those whom He loved and chose before the foundation of the world to be partakers of every spiritual blessing (Eph. 1:3–4). "The world" was specifically excluded from the saving design of His prayer.

Our prayers, however, are not the prayers of a high priest; we pray as ambassadors of Christ, whose task it is to beseech men and women on His behalf to be reconciled to God (2 Cor. 5:20). We are therefore commanded to offer our "entreaties and prayers, petitions and thanksgivings ... on behalf of all men" (1 Tim. 2:1). Our earnest desire ought to be for the salvation of all sinners (cf. Rom. 9:3; 10:1). We are not to try to limit evangelism to the elect.

There are three reasons we must not limit our evangelism. First, we are commanded to preach to everyone in the world (Matt. 28:19–20; Mark 16:15; Luke 24:46–47). Second, God's decree of election is secret. We do not know who the elect are and have no way of knowing until they respond to the gospel. Third, the scope of God's evangelistic purposes is broader than election. "Many are called, but few are chosen" (Matt. 22:14). Even Jesus' High Priestly Prayer embraces the world in this important regard. Our Lord prayed for unity among the elect so that the truth of the gospel would be made clear to the world: "that the world may believe that You sent Me ... that the world may know that You sent Me" (John 17:21,

23). God's call to all sinners is a bona fide and sincere invitation to salvation: "'As I live!' declares the Lord GOD, 'I take no pleasure in the death of the wicked, but rather that the wicked turn from his way and live. Turn back, turn back from your evil ways! Why then will you die, O house of Israel?'" (Ezek. 33:11).

Consistent with God's Desire

In some inscrutable sense, God's *desire* for the world's salvation is different from His eternal saving *purpose*. We can understand this to some degree from a human perspective; after all, our purposes frequently differ from our desires. We may *desire,* for example, to spend a day at leisure, yet a higher *purpose* compels us to go to work instead. Similarly God's saving purposes transcend His desires. (There *is* a crucial difference, of course: We might be compelled by circumstances beyond our control to choose what we do not desire. But God's choices are determined by nothing other than His own sovereign, eternal purpose.)

God genuinely "desires all men to be saved and to come to the knowledge of the truth." Yet, in "the eternal purpose which He carried out in Christ Jesus our Lord" (Eph. 3:11), He chose only the elect "out of the world" (John 17:6) and passed over the rest, leaving them to the damning consequences of their sin (cf. Rom. 1:18–32). The culpability for their damnation rests entirely on them because of their sin and rejection of God. God is not to blame for their unbelief.

Since God "desires all men to be saved," we are not required to ascertain that a person is elect before praying for that person's salvation. God alone knows who all the elect are (2 Tim. 2:19). We may pray "on behalf of all men" with full assurance that such prayers are "good and acceptable in the sight of God our Savior." After all, "The LORD is gracious and merciful; slow to anger and great in lovingkindness. The LORD is good to all, and His mercies are over all His works" (Ps. 145:8–9).

The Lord eagerly accepts prayer for the lost because it is consistent with His desire for their salvation. Such prayer is also consistent with His nature as Savior. His saving character is manifested through His Son, Jesus Christ (1 Tim. 2:5–6).

God is the "Savior of all men" in a temporal sense, but "especially of believers" in an eternal sense (1 Tim. 4:10).

When God "desires all men to be saved," He is being consistent with who He is. In Isaiah 45:22, God said, "Turn to Me and be saved, all the ends of the earth." Isaiah 55:1 invites "every one who thirsts" to "come to the waters" of salvation. Again, in Ezekiel 18:23, 32, God stated very clearly that He does not desire that the wicked should perish but that they would sincerely repent (cf. 33:11). In the New Testament, Peter wrote, "The Lord is not slow about His promise, as some count slowness, but is patient toward you, not wishing for any to perish but for all to come to repentance" (2 Peter 3:9).

No true biblical theology can teach that God takes pleasure in the damnation of the wicked. Yet, even so, God will receive glory even in the just condemnation of unbelievers (cf. Rom. 9:22–23). How His electing grace and predestined purpose can stand beside His love for the world and desire that the gospel be preached to all people, still holding them responsible for their own rejection and condemnation, is a divine mystery. The Scriptures affirm God's love for the world, His displeasure in judging sinners, His desire for all to hear the gospel and be saved. They also teach that every sinner is incapable yet responsible to believe and will be damned if he does not. Crowning the Scriptures' teaching on this matter is the great truth that God has elected all believers and loved them before the world began.

To "come to the knowledge of the truth" speaks of salvation. *Epignōsis* ("knowledge") is used four times in the Pastoral Epistles (1 Tim. 2:4; 2 Tim. 2:25; 3:7; Titus 1:1), and in each occurrence it refers to the true knowledge that brings about salvation. Far from desiring their damnation, God desires the lost to come to a saving knowledge of the truth.

Some have argued that 1 Timothy 2:3–7 teaches universalism. If God desires the salvation of all men, they argue, then all will be saved, or God won't get what He wants. Others argue that what God wills comes to pass, because "all men" refers to all classes of people, not every individual. Neither of those positions is necessary, however. We must distinguish between God's will of decree (His eternal purpose) and His will expressed as desire. *Desire* is not from *boulomai*, which would be more likely to express God's will of decree, but from *thelō*, which Paul used in 1 Timothy 2 and can refer to God's will of desire. This is precisely the distinction theologians often make between God's secret will and His revealed will.

God desires many things that He does not decree. It was never God's *desire* that sin exist; yet the undeniable existence of sin proves that even it fulfills His eternal purposes (Isa. 46:10)—though in no sense is He the author of sin (James 1:13).

Jesus lamented over Jerusalem, "Jerusalem, Jerusalem, who kills the prophets and stones those who are sent to her! How often I wanted to gather your children together, the way a hen gathers her chicks under her wings, and you were unwilling" (Matt. 23:37).

John Murray and Ned B. Stonehouse wrote, "We have found that God Himself expresses an ardent desire for the fulfillment of certain things which He has not decreed in His inscrutable counsel to come to pass."[3] God desires all men to be saved. It is their willful rejection of Him that sends them to hell. The biblical truths of election and predestination do not cancel man's moral responsibility.

Reflects the Uniqueness of God

One of the most fundamental teachings of Scripture is that "there is one God" (cf. Deut. 4:35, 39; Isa. 43:10; 1 Cor. 8:4, 6). That runs counter to the pluralistic religiosity of our world, which rejects the concept of any exclusive religious truth. We are taught by the over-tolerant spirit of our age that the gods of the Christians, Jews, Muslims, Buddhists, and Hindus are to be considered equally valid. If that were true, there would be many ways of salvation and hence no need for evangelism. But since there is only one true God, then He is the One in whom all must believe to be saved (1 Tim. 2:5). There is no other name under heaven by which sinners may be saved (Acts 4:12). Evangelistic prayer recognizes that all must come to the one true God.

Consistent with the Person of Christ

Not only is there only one God, but "one mediator also between God and men, the man Christ Jesus." *Mediator* refers to one who intervenes between two individuals to restore peace or ratify a covenant. The concept of a mediator is seen in Job's lament: "There is no umpire between us, who may lay his hand upon us both" (Job 9:33). Because Christ is the only mediator, all must come to God through

Him (Acts 4:12). There isn't an endless series of aeons, or subgods, as the Gnostics taught. We do not approach God through the intercession of angels, saints, or Mary. Only through "the man Christ Jesus" can people draw near to God. Hebrews 8:6 calls Him "the mediator of a better covenant," while Hebrews 9:15 and 12:24 describe Him as the mediator of the new covenant. Everyone who comes to God must come through Him.

Reflects the Fullness of Christ's Atonement

Our Lord freely gave His life when He died for our sins. In John 10:17–18, He said:

> For this reason the Father loves Me, because I lay down My life that I may take it again. No one has taken it away from Me, but I lay it down on My own initiative. I have authority to lay it down, and I have authority to take it up again. This commandment I received from My Father.

He voluntarily went to the cross and gave all of Himself, not merely something He possessed.

Ransom is a rich theological term describing Christ's substitutionary death for us. It is not the simple word for "ransom," *lutron*, but *antilutron*, with the added preposition intensifying the meaning. Christ did not merely pay a ransom to free us; He became the victim in our place. He died our death and bore our sin. He gave Himself.

The phrase *gave Himself as a ransom for all* is a comment on the *sufficiency* of the atonement, not its *design*. To apply a well-known epigram, the ransom paid by Christ to God for the satisfaction of His justice is sufficient for all but efficacious for the elect only. Christ's atonement is therefore unlimited as to its sufficiency but limited as to its application. Real benefits accrue "for all" because of Christ's all-sufficient atoning work. The gospel may be preached indiscriminately to all (Mark 16:15); the water of life and the offer of divine mercy are extended freely to all (Rev. 22:17); Christ is set forth as Savior for all to embrace (1 Tim. 4:10; 1 John 4:14). Moreover, in a temporal sense, when Adam and Eve sinned, the entire race was spared from immediate destruction and judgment (a privilege not afforded to the angels who fell—Heb. 2:16), and individual sinners now experience common grace and delay in God's judgment on their sins. Nineteenth-century theologian William G. T. Shedd wrote:

> The atonement is sufficient in value to expiate the sin of all men indiscriminately; and this fact should be stated because it is a fact. There are no claims of justice not yet satisfied; there is no sin of man for which an infinite atonement has not been provided.... Therefore the call to "come" is universal.[4]

That does not mean that all will be saved. Christ's death was *sufficient* to cover the sins of all men, but it is applied to the elect alone. The price paid was infinite—it was sufficient for all. "Christ's expiation ... is a divine act. It is indivisible, inexhaustible, sufficient in itself to cover the guilt of all the sins that will ever be committed on earth."[5]

Therefore salvation can sincerely and legitimately be offered to all, though only the elect will respond. Shedd continued, "The extent to which a medicine is offered is not limited by the number of persons favorably disposed to buy it and use it. Its adaptation to disease is the sole consideration in selling it, and consequently it is offered to everybody."[6]

It is crucial to understand that the atoning work of Christ fully accomplishes everything God declared He would accomplish in eternity past with regard to the salvation of sinners. God's sovereign purposes are not thwarted in any degree by the unbelief of those who spurn Christ. The atonement of Christ does not represent a failed attempt to save anyone who will not be saved. All those whom God purposed to save from eternity past will be saved (cf. John 17:12). Yet, it is worth reiterating once more that while God's saving *purpose* is limited to the elect, His *desire* for the salvation of sinners is as broad as the human race. He "desires all men to be saved and to come to the knowledge of the truth." So Christ "gave Himself as a ransom [sufficient] for all." How graphically the atoning work of Christ reveals to us the heart of God for the salvation of sinners!

That is why Paul referred to the atonement as "the testimony given [by Christ] at the proper time." This thought precisely parallels Galatians 4:4–5: "But when the fullness of the time came, God sent forth His Son, born of a woman, born under the Law, so that He might redeem those who were under the Law." Christ "gave Himself as a ransom" at exactly "the proper time" in God's redemptive plan. His redemptive work is the most eloquent testimony ever borne to God's saving desire for sinners. Evangelistic prayer for all

men therefore reflects the heart of God and honors Christ's work
on the cross.

In Accord with Paul's Divine Commission

Paul wrote, "For this I was appointed a preacher and an apostle"
(1 Tim. 2:7). Paul's divine commission was based on the great truths
that God is our Savior, Christ is our mediator, and Christ gave
Himself as a ransom, as discussed in the preceding verses. *Preacher*
derives from the verb *kērussō*, which means "to herald, proclaim, or
speak publicly." The ancient world had no news media, so announce-
ments were made in the city squares. Paul was a public herald
proclaiming the gospel of Jesus Christ. An apostle was a messenger,
sent on behalf of Christ. If the gospel message were exclusive, that
would have undercut Paul's calling.

We too are called to proclaim the gospel to the lost world. That
call, like Paul's divine commission, is based on God's desire that all be
saved. Evangelistic prayer acknowledges our responsibility.

The greatest example of evangelistic praying is our Lord Himself.
Isaiah 53:12 tells us He "interceded for the transgressors." On the
cross He prayed, "Father, forgive them; for they do not know what
they are doing" (Luke 23:34). God answered those prayers with three
thousand converts on the day of Pentecost and countless thousands
more through the centuries.

Do you pray for the lost like that? Do you have the passion that
inspired John Knox to cry out, "Give me Scotland or I die"? Is your
attitude that of George Whitefield, who prayed, "O Lord, give me
souls or take my soul"? Can you, like Henry Martyn, say, "I cannot
endure existence if Jesus is to be so dishonored"?

God honors your prayers for the lost. Standing among those who killed Stephen was a young man named Saul of Tarsus. Could it be that the great apostle's salvation was in answer to Stephen's prayer, "Lord, do not hold this sin against them!" (Acts 7:60)? Evangelism begins with prayer.

Are you prepared to be alone with God? You are now armed to go into His presence with much to talk about. Jesus has given you the pattern to use, and the apostle Paul has provided you with a list of priorities. I hope you'll discover real power and passion as you pray according to these realities. As a result, may you grow to be more like Christ and to see many of the elect enter into the kingdom.

DISCUSSION GUIDE

For Personal Study

Settle into your favorite chair with your Bible, a pen or pencil, and this book. Read a chapter of this book, marking portions that seem significant to you. Write in the margins. Note where you agree, disagree, or question the author. Look up the referenced Scripture passages. Then turn to the questions listed in this discussion guide. If you want to trace your progress with a written record, use a notebook to record your answers, thoughts, feelings, and further questions. Refer to the text and to the Scriptures as you allow the questions to enlarge your thinking. And *pray.* Ask God to give you a discerning mind for truth, an active concern for others, and a greater love for Himself.

For Group Study
Plan Ahead

Before meeting with your group, read and mark the chapter as if you were preparing for personal study. Glance through the questions, making mental notes of how you might contribute to your group's discussion. Bring a Bible and the text to your meeting.

Arrange an Environment That Promotes Discussion

Comfortable chairs arranged in a casual circle invite people to talk with each other. Then say, "We are here to listen and respond to each other—and to learn together." If you are the leader, simply be sure to sit where you can have eye contact with each person.

Promptness Counts

Time is as valuable to many people as money. If the group runs late (because of a late start), these people will feel as robbed as if you had picked their pockets. So, unless you have a mutual agreement, begin and end on time.

Involve Everyone

Group learning works best if everyone participates more or less equally. If you are a natural *talker*, pause before you enter the conversation. Then ask a quiet person what he or she thinks. If you are a natural *listener*, don't hesitate to jump into the discussion. Others will benefit from your thoughts—but only if you speak them. If you are the *leader*, be careful not to dominate the session. Of course, you will have thought about the study ahead of time, but don't assume that people are present just to hear you—as flattering as that may feel. Instead, help group members make their own discoveries. Ask the questions, but insert your own ideas only as they are needed to fill gaps.

Pace the Study

The questions for each session are designed to last about one hour. Early questions form the framework for later discussion, so don't rush by so quickly that you miss a valuable foundation. Later questions, however, often speak of the here and now. Thus don't dawdle so long at the beginning that you leave no time to "get personal." While the leader must take responsibility for timing the flow of questions, it is the job of each person in the group to assist in keeping the study moving at an even pace.

Pray for Each Other—Together or Alone

Then watch God's hand at work in all of your lives. Notice that each session includes the following features:

Session Topic—a brief statement summarizing the session.

Community Builder—an activity to get acquainted with the session topic and/or with each other.

Questions—a list of questions to encourage individual or group discovery and application.

Prayer Focus—suggestions for turning one's learning into prayer.

Optional Activities—supplemental ideas that will enhance the study.

Assignment—activities or preparation to complete prior to the next session.

1

A HEART SET ON GOD

Session Topic
A believer whose heart is set on God will cultivate a constant attitude of prayer throughout each day.

Community Builder (Choose One)
1. Today's society presents us with many options for how to spend our free time. Name one activity you like to do for leisure. Do you think this ever consumes too much of your time?

2. Are you a morning or an evening person? Or does time of day not affect your alertness? How does your answer influence when you spend extended time in prayer?

Group Discovery Questions

1. Is breathing a good illustration of what prayer ought to be like? Why or why not?

2. Why would any Christian want to behave like a practical humanist? Name and discuss several things (programs, methods, resources) that you think could lead to such action.

3. How did the miraculous events on the day of Pentecost affect the prayer practices of the early church (Acts 1—2; 6:4)?

4. What did you envision when you first heard the statement "Pray without ceasing"? Was this different from your current understanding of 1 Thessalonians 5:17? If so, how?

5. How does the wording at the beginning of Ephesians 6:18 help explain the all-encompassing nature of prayer?

6. What two important but contrasting lessons can we learn from the prayer time in the garden of Gethsemane (Matt. 26:36–46; Luke 22:40–46)?

7. How are the parables in Luke 11:5–10 and 18:1–8 different from the other ones Jesus told?

8. What is so significant about praying "in the Spirit"? (See Rom. 8:26–27.)

Prayer Focus

- Pray that, as you start this study, God would help you and each member of your group to become more aware of the need for daily prayer.

- Resolve to set aside enough time at the end of each meeting to pray as a group and follow up on previous weeks' prayer requests.

Optional Activities

1. Reread the long quotation from Charles Spurgeon in the section titled "A Way of Life." Try rewriting it in more contemporary language. Use at least one modern illustration that would exemplify the truth of how prayer ought to be a way of life.

2. Keep a prayer journal over the next month. Record lists of things and people you need to pray for. Also leave room for writing down answers to prayer. Share with a Christian friend at least one of the answers the Lord gives.

Assignment

1. Memorize Ephesians 6:18.

2. Read chapter 2 of *Alone with God.*

2

SEEKING THE LORD IN SECRET

Session Topic

God wants us to approach Him in prayer with humility, openness, and sincerity, not with pride and hypocrisy like the Pharisees.

Community Builder (Choose One)

1. Share what your favorite kind of getaway spot is (one where you can be alone). Some might want to describe more specifically where theirs is and what it's like.

2. We all dislike insincerity and contrived approaches in everyday life. Can you think of an experience (perhaps with an overzealous salesperson) that was especially irritating for you?

Group Discovery Questions

1. What was the Old Testament view of the importance of prayer? (See Ps. 65:2; 91:15; 145:18.)

2. How did the prophet Isaiah model the trait of reverence when he was face-to-face with God? (See Isa. 6.)

3. Did the Jews have a sense of solidarity? If so, what was it based on, and how did it affect their prayer lives?

4. What were some characteristics and attitudes of ritualized prayer? What are the names of the two most common formal prayers used by the Jews?

5. Do you have the tendency to offer public prayers that are too long? If so, look again at Jesus' warning in Mark 12:40 and consider some ways you might streamline your prayers.

6. What sin was at the heart of the Pharisees' approach to prayer (Matt. 6:5)?

7. What prayer trait did the Jews borrow from the Gentiles? Did it enhance or detract from the content of prayers offered to God?

Prayer Focus

- Set aside some time during the coming week to examine your motives for prayer. Ask God to reveal to you the things that may hinder your regular prayer times.

- Do you have a quiet place where you can go to pray? If not, ask God to provide a spot where you can get away from everything else and be with Him. If you have such a place, thank Him for providing it.

- The discipline of daily prayer can become monotonous. Ask the Lord to give you renewed strength and fresh desire to be faithful in prayer.

Optional Activities

1. Go to your church library or local Christian bookstore and obtain another book about prayer. Read it over the next few weeks and write down those things that might supplement the theme of *Alone with God*.

2. Most of us receive at least a couple of prayer letters from missionaries or Christian ministries. Reread several recent ones and evaluate them on how well they present their prayer requests. Do you feel they are self-centered, or do they seek to put the attention on God? Write down your thoughts.

Assignment

1. Read Matthew 6:8–13 and Luke 11:1–4. Notice the differences in context and wording of the Lord's Prayer.

2. Read chapter 3 of *Alone with God*.

3

"OUR FATHER"

Session Topic

Prayer should always begin and end with the recognition that we can and ought to glorify God as our Father.

Community Builder (Choose One)

1. Some church traditions recite the Lord's Prayer every week as part of the worship service. Do you think this practice is scriptural? Why or why not?

2. Several years ago, Bible commentator J. B. Phillips wrote a book titled *Your God Is Too Small*. Do people still expect too little of God today? Or do they make too many demands of Him when praying?

Group Discovery Questions

1. What great truth did Jonah, Daniel, and Jeremiah exemplify in their prayers? Look again at Jonah 2, Daniel 9, and Jeremiah 32.

2. What is a more accurate title we could give to the Lord's Prayer?

3. Reconstruct one of the outlines or patterns of the prayer that you believe best shows Jesus' purpose in sharing it with the disciples. Why do you favor the one you chose?

4. What distinguishes the children of light from the children of darkness? (See Eph. 5:8; 2 Peter 1:4.)

5. What five elements encompassed the fatherhood of God for Old Testament Jews? To which one or ones do you think believers today can most easily relate?

6. What word for father did Jesus often use when referring to God? What does it mean in English?

7. Read Matthew 7:7–11 again. What do you find most helpful or comforting from this passage?

8. What are the benefits of having God as our Father? How would you arrange them in order of importance?

Prayer Focus

- Not everyone has a good relationship with (or good memories of) his or her earthly father. Pray and thank God that He is always available to be a loving Heavenly Father.

- What has been the focus of your recent prayer times? If it has been too self-centered, ask the Lord to help your prayer be more centered on Him.

Optional Activities

1. Do a brief study of the person and attributes of God. Read a standard work on the subject, such as A. W. Tozer's *The Knowledge of the Holy* or Arthur W. Pink's *The Attributes of God*. Take some notes on your reading and tell the group what was most profitable from your study.

2. Read Psalm 139 and meditate on what it says about God's omnipresence and omniscience. Record some key verses to remember.

Assignment

1. Begin memorizing Matthew 6:9–13.

2. Read chapter 4 of *Alone with God*.

4

"HALLOWED BE YOUR NAME"

Session Topic

When Christians approach God in prayer, they are to remind themselves of His holiness and the greatness of His name.

Community Builder (Choose One)

1. How do you respond when you hear someone use the Lord's name in vain? Do you think, as a rule, it is better just to ignore the remark or to admonish the person?

2. People's names are important to them. Share, if you can, some interesting fact about your name or the selection of a child's name.

Group Discovery Questions

1. What is the primary reason for the existence of the church and each individual within it?

2. What is the most familiar Hebrew name for God? (See Ex. 3:14.) Why did the Jews not say that name out loud?

3. In Scripture, names were more than mere titles. What more important thing are they representative of or equated with?

4. How did Jesus reveal God's character to His disciples? (See John 1:14; 14:9.)

5. What Old Testament verse lists more names for Jesus Christ than any New Testament verse?

6. What contemporary words can be used as synonyms for *hallowed?* What do they tell us about our relationship with God?

7. What is the most central truth, or most important attribute, concerning God (Isa. 6:3)?

8. Nine "anxieties of holiness" are listed under the section titled "The Fear of the Lord Is Not an Option." Which ones do you think are the most difficult to deal with and why?

9. What three truths must be grasped in order to fully "hallow" God's name?

Prayer Focus

- How has your zeal for the dignity of God's name and your progress in the pursuit of your own sanctification been lately? Spend some time in prayer reviewing your attitudes. Ask God to forgive your indifference and increase your desire to know Him.

- How respectful are you of the good names (reputations) of fellow Christians, especially those who are leaders in your church? Pray that you would be faithful in this regard and that those leaders would present good testimonies in the community.

Optional Activities

1. Write each Hebrew name for God, with its English translation, on a separate piece of paper or index card. Try memorizing the meanings of all eleven terms. Look up and record the Old Testament passages in which they are used.

2. Have you ever experienced an "anxiety of holiness"? It could have occurred when you became a Christian or at some later date. Give a short testimony to that experience at your next study meeting. You might want to recount someone else's experience (one who is not part of your present group) if you feel that it is more appropriate or timelier. If you do not share a testimony with the group,

write out your recollections as a prayer or "open letter" of thankfulness to God.

Assignment

1. Continue to work on memorizing Matthew 6:9–13. Review some portion of it every day.

2. Read chapter 5 of *Alone with God*.

5

"YOUR KINGDOM COME"

Session Topic
Our prayers should support the establishment of God's kingdom and the rule of Christ within it.

Community Builder (Choose One)
1. What is one thing about today's American culture that greatly concerns you? How does this thing contribute to the post-Christian or anti-Christian atmosphere in our country?

2. Do you have any future plans or visions for your career, your family, or your personal improvement? How does the amount of time spent on those hopes compare

with the time you give to church and furthering God's kingdom? Is it hard to maintain a balance?

Group Discovery Questions

1. What is the church's chief mission in this world? What kinds of influences seek to divert it from that mission?

2. Is it valid for a Christian to bring his or her own concerns and causes before God in prayer? What is the only thing that gives them validity?

3. What poses the greatest opposition to Christ's kingdom and Christian living?

4. What is a common characteristic of all the great empires that have existed throughout world history?

5. Of the three temporal aspects—past, present, and future—of God's kingdom, which is to be our main focus in prayer?

6. What can help us reconcile the seemingly contrasting truths that God's kingdom can be present now but also coming in the future?

7. What are the two main features related to the kingdom's coming to earth now?

Prayer Focus

- Pray for our nation and its culture. Ask God to turn people's hearts away from sin and toward Him.

- Thank God for the wonderful privilege of being a member of His kingdom. Pray for several people by name whom you know are not part of God's kingdom.

- What are your priorities in relation to serving in and helping further God's kingdom? If they need to be more in line with God's, ask Him for the wisdom and guidance to make the necessary adjustments.

Optional Activities

1. Do some additional study on the nature of God's kingdom. For a view of how the kingdom contrasts with the world's system, read Martyn Lloyd-Jones' *Studies in the Sermon on the Mount,* focusing especially on the chapters dealing with Matthew 6—7. For guidance on how believers ought to live in God's kingdom today, read my book *Kingdom Living Here and Now.*

2. Read and study the parables of the kingdom in Matthew 13:1–52. Summarize in your own words the theme or themes of the passage. Record the similarities and differences you notice among the various kingdom parables.

Assignment

1. Review your memorization work on Matthew 6:9–13. Begin learning Psalm 2:6–8 as well.

2. Read chapter 6 of *Alone with God*.

6

"YOUR WILL BE DONE"

Session Topic

When we pray, our wills are to agree with God's will, and we are to desire for His will to be accomplished throughout the world.

Community Builder (Choose One)

1. How have you tended to see the effects of your prayers: more from the standpoint of your own persuasiveness or from the standpoint of how God answered your petitions? Explain your answer.

2. Describe a recent example of how you strongly wanted your own way in a situation. Did your attitude create difficulties for you or others?

Group Discovery Questions

1. How did David (Ps. 40:8) and Jesus (John 4:34) show that they were familiar with the attitude of the third petition?

2. How would you describe poet Omar Khayyám's view of God? Think of one or two adjectives that would be appropriate.

3. What does the story in Acts 12 tell us about the vulnerability of the early church's prayer life? (See esp. vv. 1–17.)

4. In regard to life's course of events, what tension has always existed between God and man? How have you resolved this tension in your own mind?

5. How and when did Jesus demonstrate a sense of righteous rebellion regarding God's will?

6. When it comes to seeing a difference or having a change occur, how do most Christians view prayer? What attitude needs to replace this view?

7. What three aspects of God's will are discussed toward the end of this chapter? Name one or two main distinctives of each aspect.

8. How can prayer be a means of progressive sanctification? Can you think of an example when it worked that way in your life or in the life of a loved one?

Prayer Focus

- Pray and ask God to conform your heart and mind to His will in everything. If you are struggling with His will in a certain situation, pray about that especially.

- Is there a violation against God's will about which your action could make a positive difference? If so, pray for wisdom and courage to take the appropriate action.

- Spend some time next week thanking God for the many ways His will is being accomplished around the world.

Optional Activities

1. Do some additional study on God's purposes in permitting evil. Read pages 105–124 of my book *The Vanishing Conscience* and write down the key points of that section.

2. Read Philip Keller's *A Layman Looks at the Lord's Prayer*. Be alert for topics of discussion that are additional to those covered in *Alone with God*.

Assignment

1. Memorize Romans 12:1–2.

2. Read chapter 7 of *Alone with God*.

7

"GIVE US THIS DAY OUR DAILY BREAD"

Session Topic

Because God has promised to provide all our physical needs, we can pray confidently and thankfully to Him that He will supply these provisions each day.

Community Builder (Choose One)

1. Most of us have some dreams about owning material goods that would be additional to our daily essentials. Is it wrong to pray for such things?

2. Has there been any time recently when you were not in a position of relative abundance? If so, what were some ways the Lord met your needs for daily bread?

Group Discovery Questions

1. What is a believer's dependence on God analogous to in a family context?

2. What kinds of needs does the term *bread* encompass?

3. What are some practical and commonplace ways people deny that God is the source of all they have?

4. Is concern for the environment and for technological tools to manage natural resources unhealthy? How can we balance these concerns with the recognition that everything we have is from God?

5. What fact makes the title of this chapter a valid petition? (See Ps. 37:3–4, 10–11, 25.)

6. How have non-Christian religions generally contributed to the lack of daily bread in some parts of the world? What specific example is given in this chapter?

7. God can certainly provide for us through miraculous means, but how does He normally supply our needs (2 Thess. 3:10–12)?

Prayer Focus

- Do you know of missionaries who might be struggling to meet their own daily needs or the daily needs of the people to whom they minister? Set aside some special time to pray for them today.

- Pray that God would help you and others in your study group live one day at a time and trust God to meet your daily needs.

- Give thanks to the Lord that He has given you, His child, all the basic provisions you need.

Optional Activities

1. Do a brief study of 2 Corinthians 9. Review the ways you are sharing your resources and making spiritual investments for God's work. Do you need to improve your efforts or add some that you have been omitting?

2. Volunteer some of your time in the coming weeks to a local food pantry, homeless shelter, or similar agency. (If your community has none of these, pray for an opportunity to help a family in your church who may be in need of material support.)

Assignment

1. Try reciting all of Matthew 6:9–13. If you're not quite ready, continue to review and memorize.

2. Read chapter 8 of *Alone with God*.

8

"FORGIVE US OUR DEBTS"

Session Topic

Because Christians continue to sin, we need to pray daily for the forgiveness of sins that only God, our loving Father, can provide.

Community Builder (Choose One)

1. What do you find to be the most intolerable character trait in others? What could make it easier to deal with such persons and forgive them?

2. When is the last time you felt great relief at having a financial debt paid off? Describe your experience. What lessons can you draw from this and apply to spiritual forgiveness?

Group Discovery Questions

1. What twofold reason makes God's forgiveness of our sins so significant for us? How does the quote from John Stott relate to this reason?

2. What six negative effects does sin have on our spiritual well-being? What other bad side effects does it have on our physical health and social well-being?

3. What five Greek words are most often used to denote the various aspects of sin? Which word or words best capture the meaning to you?

4. Describe in your own words the magnitude of God's judicial forgiveness. To whom is such forgiveness available?

5. Why do believers still have a need for God's parental forgiveness?

6. What important truths does Jesus' act of foot washing symbolize?

7. What benefits do we receive when we confess our sins? What happens when we do not? What makes confession so hard?

8. What simple principle shows us that forgiving others is the ultimate test for Christians?

9. Seven reasons for forgiving others are presented in this chapter. Which three do you and your group think are

most significant? As a group, discuss your reasoning and look at relevant Scripture verses.

Prayer Focus

- Give thanks to the Lord for His marvelous solution to the problem of sin.

- The apostle Paul told us to examine ourselves (2 Cor. 13:5). This is especially appropriate to do before partaking of the Lord's Supper. Before the next observance of Communion at your church, examine your heart and bring any unconfessed sins before the Lord for His forgiveness.

- How is your forgiving spirit toward other Christians? If there is a grudge or unconfessed sin between you and another believer, ask for forgiveness now and pray for the opportunity to make things right with the other person.

Optional Activities

1. Read John Stott's book *Confess Your Sins*. Record your comments, thoughts, and questions as you read. Write a brief synopsis of the book's theme and main points.

2. Do a word study of *forgiveness* or one of the terms for sin. If possible, use a dictionary of New Testament words, a

Bible encyclopedia, or a dictionary of theology as well as a concordance.

Assignment

1. Read and meditate on Matthew 18. Notice the many admonitions it contains about sin, confession, and forgiveness.

2. Review Matthew 6:9–13. Are you able to recite it easily?

3. Read chapter 9 of *Alone with God.*

9

"DELIVER US FROM EVIL"

Session Topic

It is all right for us to ask God to protect us from sin as we encounter life's various trials and troubles.

Community Builder (Choose One)

1. What do you believe is the biggest challenge from the world that keeps Christians from succeeding in their walks with God? What are some reasons for your answer?

2. On a scale of 0 to 10, how would you rate yourself in confronting difficulties and dangers? 0: You try to avoid confrontation whenever possible because you always seem to fail. 10: You look forward to such challenges and

wish more would come your way. Or are you somewhere in between?

Group Discovery Questions

1. What kind of word is the Greek for "temptation" in Matthew 6:13? How does it differ from the English connotation?

2. How can we best reconcile what the sixth petition says with the admonitions and explanations in James 1?

3. Does every trial necessarily have to turn into a temptation? If not, what is the key factor that prevents this from happening?

4. What common thread of truth runs through Job 23:10; 1 Corinthians 10:13; and 1 Peter 1:6–7?

5. What is the ultimate key in dealing successfully with temptation? (See Ps. 119:11; James 4:7.)

Prayer Focus

• Thank the Lord that, by the Holy Spirit's power, evil is restrained from being even more rampant than it already is.

• Do you have an ongoing struggle with a particular temptation or sin? Lay claim to the promise in

1 Corinthians 10:13 and ask God for strength to resist temptation the next time it comes.

Optional Activities

1. Do a comparative study of Matthew 4:1–11 and Luke 4:1–13, two accounts of Jesus' temptation in the desert. Notice the similarity between the accounts. What Old Testament references do both passages quote?

2. Over the next month during your personal devotional time, look for verses that attest to the power of God's Word to overcome evil. Make a list of these verses and select several for memorization. (Try to include this exercise in your regular reading and study time.)

Assignment

1. Complete your memorization work on Matthew 6:9–13. Review it as many times as necessary in order to recite it at your next group study.

2. Read chapter 10 of *Alone with God.*

10

PRAYING FOR THE RIGHT THINGS

Session Topic

If we are truly praying for the right things, we will focus our prayer requests on what pertains to God's kingdom and our own spiritual growth.

Community Builder (Choose One)

1. What two or three categories most typically dominate the prayer requests offered during the average church prayer meeting? Are most requests in line with God's priorities?

2. How would you assess your value system right now regarding possessions? What item(s) would be especially hard to give up? Is there something else that would be easy to do without?

Group Discovery Questions

1. What kind of disillusionment came to the young lawyer in the Anton Chekhov story? What happened as a result of his disenchantment?

2. Throughout the recorded prayers of the apostle Paul, what was his primary concern?

3. In Paul's epistles, what does the phrase *your calling* always refer to?

4. What basic area does the concept of worthiness encompass? What are some practical ways in which you could test your own worthiness?

5. Why is it so important for Christians to walk worthily? What are some of the negative results of not walking worthily?

6. How could David be so bold in his desire for true spiritual fulfillment?

7. What is a primary reason that many unbelievers continue to reject Christianity? How can we behave so that people around us do not reject the truth? (See Matt. 5:16.)

Prayer Focus

• Our prayer requests are often off target from what God would want them to be. Review the main things you have prayed for recently. Eliminate those that are self-centered, and ask God to help you focus on the right things.

• Spend some time thanking the Lord that He is concerned about your spiritual growth and that He provides resources to assist in that growth.

• Each day during the coming week pray for a different person in your group that he or she would walk worthy of the Christian profession.

Optional Activities

1. The New Testament contains thirty-three prayers of the apostle Paul. Pick out at least ten of these to read and study in more depth. (Many of them are fairly brief.) Make a list of the key elements contained in Paul's prayers.

2. Refer to the list of characteristics that manifest a worthy Christian walk. Choose seven (one for each day of the week) and write them, along with their verses, on individual index cards. Meditate on one each day next week.

Assignment

1. Memorize one of the verses from the list of worthy-walk traits.

2. Read chapter 11 of *Alone with God*.

11

PRAYING FOR THE LOST

Session Topic
In order to be involved in reaching the lost, we first need to understand the essentials of evangelistic praying.

Community Builder (Choose One)
1. Do you find it difficult to pray for those in authority, such as world and national leaders? Why is it easy to forget such people in our prayers?

2. Sometimes people are converted to Christ after being the subject of prayers for many years. If someone in your group knows the details of such a case, have them share it with the entire group.

Group Discovery Questions

1. What expression in Romans 9:1–4 demonstrates the apostle Paul's strong desire to see his fellow Jews saved?

2. What are the four terms Paul uses in 1 Timothy 2:1 concerning evangelistic praying? Give an example of how the different shades of meaning could be applied to various needs.

3. What are several ways that praying for the salvation of *all* the lost is consistent with God's heart? (See Ezek. 33:11; Acts 17:30; 1 Tim. 2:4.)

4. Has the political activism of some Christian groups in recent years made any difference in reaching the lost? What truth from 2 Corinthians 10:4 is often forgotten?

5. What favorable conditions in our nation and society will the church and individual believers see as a result of faithfulness in evangelistic prayer?

6. How is our task of praying for the lost different from Jesus' prayer in John 17? (Compare v. 9 with 2 Cor. 5:20.)

7. How ought God's eternal saving purpose, coupled with His desire that no one perish, be a comfort to us in our praying for and witnessing to the lost? (See 2 Tim. 2:19.)

8. How should the uniqueness of God give us incentive to pray for the lost?

9. Spend some time discussing the nature of Christ's atonement. How can it be unlimited in sufficiency but limited in application?

10. Upon what truths was Paul's commission as an apostle and preacher based? How does that relate to the responsibility God has given us?

Prayer Focus

• How diligent have you been during the past year to pray for unsaved friends and relatives? Ask the Lord to help you maintain or if necessary, improve your efforts.

• Choose the name of one unsaved person, perhaps a family member, and devote extra time during the coming month to praying for his or her salvation.

• Express your thanks to God for His great salvation and for His marvelous love in drawing you to Himself.

Optional Activities

1. Read J. I. Packer's *Evangelism and the Sovereignty of God* or Charles Spurgeon's *The Soul Winner*. Look for insights on how you can apply what the book says to your evangelistic activities (witnessing as well as praying).

2. If you know a missionary pastor who is engaged in church planting, write him a letter and tell him of your prayer support. Share some of the principles you learned in this chapter and assure him of your prayers for the people he is seeking to reach with the Lord's help.

Assignment

1. Review your memory work on Matthew 6:9–13. Try to finish memorizing it in the next week or two if you were unable to complete the assignment earlier.

2. Begin memorizing 1 Timothy 2:1–6. Give yourself a goal for when you will have the complete passage learned.

NOTES

Introduction

1. Martyn Lloyd-Jones, *Studies in the Sermon on the Mount* (Grand Rapids, MI: Eerdmans, 1979), 2:45.

2. J. Oswald Sanders, *Effective Prayer* (Chicago: Moody, 1969), 7.

3. Lloyd-Jones, *Sermon on the Mount*, 2:45.

4. John MacArthur Jr., *Jesus' Pattern of Prayer* (Chicago: Moody, 1981).

Chapter 1: A Heart Set on God

1. Charles Haddon Spurgeon, *The Parables of Our Lord* (Grand Rapids, MI: Baker, 1979), 434–35.

2. E. M. Bounds, *Purpose in Prayer* (Chicago: Moody, n.d.), 53–54.

3. Spurgeon, *Parables of Our Lord*, 436–37.

Chapter 2: Seeking the Lord in Secret

1. John Preston, *The Puritans on Prayer* (Morgan, PA: Soli Deo Gloria, 1995), 25–26.

2. Lloyd-Jones, *Sermon on the Mount*, 2:22–23.

3. William Barclay, *The Gospel of Matthew* (Philadelphia: Westminster, 1958), 1:191–98.

Chapter 3: "Our Father"

1. Bounds, *Purpose in Prayer*, 43.

2. John Stott, *Christian CounterCulture: The Message of the Sermon on the Mount* (Downers Grove, IL: InterVarsity, 1979), 151–52.

3. Paul Tournier, *A Doctor's Casebook in the Light of the Bible*, cited in William Barclay, *The Beatitudes and the Lord's Prayer for Every Man* (New York: Harper & Row, 1963), 172.

4. Arthur W. Pink, *An Exposition of the Sermon on the Mount* (Grand Rapids, MI: Baker, 1950), 161.

Chapter 4: "Hallowed Be Your Name"

1. Lloyd-Jones, *Sermon on the Mount*, 2:60–61.

2. Pink, *Exposition Sermon*, 161–62.

3. John Calvin, cited in *A Harmony of the Gospels Matthew, Mark, and Luke* (Grand Rapids, MI: Baker, 1979), 318.

4. Immanuel Kant, cited by William Barclay, *The Gospel of Matthew* (Philadelphia: Westminster, 1975), 1:208.

5. Origen, Contra Celsus, book 1, chapter 25.

Chapter 5: "Your Kingdom Come"

1. James Orr, cited by Alva J. McClain, *The Greatness of the Kingdom* (Winona Lake, IN: BMH, 1980), 22.

Chapter 6: "Your Will Be Done"

1. James Montgomery Boice, *The Sermon on the Mount* (Grand Rapids, MI: Zondervan, 1972), 183–84.

2. William Barclay, *The Gospel of Matthew* (Philadelphia: Westminster, 1975), 1:212.

3. For a more detailed treatment of this topic, please see my book *The Vanishing Conscience* (Dallas: Word, 1994), 105–24.

4. David Wells, "Prayer: Rebelling against the Status Quo," *Christianity Today,* November 2, 1979, 33.

5. John Hannah, "Prayer and the Sovereignty of God," *Bibliotheca Sacra,* October–December 1979, 353.

6. Philip Keller, *A Layman Looks at the Lord's Prayer* (Chicago: Moody, 1985), 92–97.

Chapter 7: "Give Us This Day Our Daily Bread"

1. Lloyd-Jones, *Sermon on the Mount,* 2:68–69.

2. Stott, *Christian CounterCulture,* 149.

3. Thomas Watson, *The Lord's Prayer* (London: Banner of Truth Trust, 1972), 197.

Chapter 8: "Forgive Us Our Debts"

1. Henry Ward Beecher, cited in *Encyclopedia of 2585 Illustrations* (Grand Rapids, MI: Zondervan, n.d.), 260.

2. John Stott, *Confess Your Sins* (Waco, TX: Word, 1974), 73.

3. Pink, *Exposition Sermon,* 163–64.

4. For an in-depth treatment of this critical topic, please refer to my book *Faith Works* (Dallas: Word, 1993), 87–104.

5. Donald Grey Barnhouse, *God's Methods for Holy Living* (Grand Rapids, MI: Eerdmans, 1951), 72–74.

6. Stott, *Confess Your Sins,* 19.

Chapter 10: Praying for the Right Things

1. Donald S. Whitney, *Spiritual Disciplines for the Christian Life* (Colorado Springs, CO: NavPress, 1991), 115–16.

Chapter 11: Praying for the Lost

1. Charles Haddon Spurgeon, *The Soul Winner* (Grand Rapids, MI: Eerdmans, 1989), 246–47.

2. Richard Baxter, cited in I. D. E. Thomas, ed., *A Puritan Golden Treasury* (Edinburgh, Scotland: Banner of Truth, 1977), 92–93.

3. John Murray and Ned B. Stonehouse, *The Free Offer of the Gospel* (Phillipsburg, NJ: Presbyterian and Reformed, 1979), 26.

4. William G. T. Shedd, *Dogmatic Theology*, (Nashville, TN: Thomas Nelson, 1980), 2:482.

5. R. L. Dabney, *The Five Points of Calvinism* (Harrisonburg, VA: Sprinkle, 1992), 61.

6. Shedd, *Dogmatic Theology*, 2:482.